Jesus' 12 GREATEST QUESTIONS

Most of these studies were adapted from the transcripts of lessons taught at the Polishing the Pulpit Workshop in Sevierville, Tennessee, in 2024. Listen to the original lessons from PTP by scanning the QR code or by going to feeds.captivate.fm/jesus-12-greatest/.

POLISHING THE
PULPIT

Table of Contents

Introduction
Allen Webster (Page 1)

Introduction

Allen Webster

What Do You Think of the Christ?

Jesus asked the Pharisees, "What do you think about the Christ?" (Matthew 22:42). This is history's most important question—and eternity's most decisive one. Was Jesus just a man, or is He God in the flesh? This lesson walks through evidence of Jesus' divinity: fulfilled prophecy, sinless life, miracles, and resurrection. You cannot be neutral. He is Lord, liar, or lunatic. If He is Lord, then He must be followed. The sermon presses for confession—not just with lips, but with life. Believing is not enough—faith must lead to obedience. What you think of Christ determines where you spend forever.

By What Authority Do You Do These Things?

Jesus was asked, "By what authority are You doing these things?" (Matthew 21:23). He answered with a question about John's baptism—from heaven or men? God's people must answer the same today: Do our practices come from divine revelation or human tradition? Authority matters in doctrine, worship, and daily living. The Pharisees had authority issues—they would not submit to heaven's will. Many still ask the right questions but reject the right answers. This sermon affirms the Bible as our only authority, calling us to restore New Testament Christianity—not by creed, culture, or convenience, but by "Thus saith the Lord."

What Do You Do More Than Others?

Jesus inquired, "What do you do more than others?" (Matthew 5:47). God's people are called to go the second mile. Anyone can love friends. Christians must love enemies. Anyone can greet brothers. Christians greet strangers. This question presses us beyond complacency. Are we just good, or are we Christlike? The world does not need average believers. It needs extraordinary disciples. This lesson urges more compassion, more holiness, more sacrifice. Because Jesus did more than others—we must, too. Heaven is not for the lukewarm, but the devoted. Go further. Give more. Serve better. Shine brighter. That is what sets the church apart.

What Is the Kingdom of God Like?

Jesus compared the kingdom to a mustard seed (Luke 13:18–19). It begins small—just a whisper of faith, a handful of disciples—but it grows into a mighty tree. This lesson highlights the power of spiritual beginnings. The church began with fishermen in an upper room. Today, it shelters souls across the globe. Like the seed, it grows quietly, steadily, until its branches reach every nation. And like the birds in the parable, weary souls find shelter in its arms. Do not despise small things. The kingdom is growing—in hearts, in homes, in hard places. Plant. Water. Trust God with the increase.

What Do You Seek?

Jesus asked His first followers, "What do you seek?" (John 1:38). This is the question behind every action. Some seek success. Others seek security. But wise souls seek the Savior. This sermon uncovers the heart behind discipleship. Following Jesus starts with desire. What are you truly hungry for? The world offers empty promises. But Christ offers truth, peace, and eternal life. The lesson calls us to honest evaluation: Are we following Jesus because we need Him—or because we want something from Him? The only pursuit that satisfies the soul is the pursuit of Christ. Ask. Seek. Knock. He will be found.

What Will It Profit?

Jesus asked, "What will it profit a man if he gains the whole world, and loses his own soul?" (Mark 8:36). This lesson reminds us of the eternal imbalance between earthly gain and spiritual loss. Careers, fame, riches—all are worthless at death. Your soul is your most precious possession. Many trade an eternity of joy for a moment of pleasure. But no amount of wealth can buy back a lost soul. Jesus gave His life to save ours. This question is heaven's wake-up call: What is truly valuable to you? The only wise exchange is the world for Christ—not the other way around.

Will He Find Faith?

Jesus posed a soul-searching question: "When the Son of Man comes, will He really find faith on the earth?" (Luke 18:8). The world may grow darker. The church may grow smaller. But God's faithful must not grow silent. This lesson

What Do You Think of the Christ?

The Divine Question of Identity and Eternity

Kyle Butt

"While the Pharisees were gathered together, Jesus asked them, saying, 'What do you think about the Christ? Whose Son is He?' They said to Him, 'The Son of David.' "

—MATTHEW 22:41–42

A Dangerous Answer

Imagine being asked a question so dangerous, so radical, that answering it truthfully could cost you your life. Every year, thousands of Christians around the globe are persecuted, even executed, for one confession: *Jesus Christ is the Son of God.*

This is no theoretical matter. In 2002, six believers in Pakistan were taken by gunmen, bound, gagged, and shot—all because they affirmed their belief in Jesus Christ as the Son of God. The question that cost them their lives is the same question Jesus once asked the religious leaders of His day: "What do you think about the Christ? Whose Son is He?" (Matthew 22:42).

This question remains the most consequential inquiry in all of human history. It is not merely academic; it is deeply personal. It confronts every individual with the identity of Jesus and the implications of that identity for their lives.

The Setting: A Silenced Crowd

Matthew 22 records a remarkable series of confrontations. The Pharisees, Sadducees, and scribes—the religious elite—each took turns trying to trap Jesus. They posed questions about taxes, the resurrection, and the greatest commandment. With wisdom and authority, Jesus silenced them all.

Finally, Jesus turned the tables. He asked a question of His own. Not a trick, not a trap—but a test of understanding and belief: "What do you think of the Christ? Whose Son is He?" (Matthew 22:42).

Their answer: "The Son of David."

This was a correct but incomplete answer. The Messiah was prophesied to come from David's lineage (Isaiah 9:6-7; Jeremiah 23:5). But Jesus was not merely David's descendant—He was David's Lord.

This was a pivotal moment. The Pharisees prided themselves on knowing the Scriptures. They had read Psalm 110 countless times. But they had missed its deeper meaning. Jesus was inviting them—and us—to see beyond the surface, to understand that the Messiah is divine.

More Than a Man

Jesus pressed the point. He quoted Psalm 110:1, written by David: "The LORD said to my Lord, 'Sit at My right hand, till I make Your enemies Your footstool.'" If David called Him "Lord," how could He also be his son?

This was a question the religious leaders could not answer. From that moment, they dared not question Him further (Matthew 22:46).

Jesus was pointing them to a mystery made clear only through faith: The Christ is both fully human and fully divine. He is the root and offspring of David (Revelation 22:16). He existed before David and yet came through David's lineage.

This doctrine is central to Christianity. If Jesus were only a man, His death would have no power to save. But as the Son of God, His blood is able to redeem the world (1 Peter 1:18-19). To misunderstand the identity of Christ is to miss salvation itself.

The Trilemma: Lord, Liar, or Lunatic

C. S. Lewis once observed that one cannot merely call Jesus a great moral teacher. A man who claimed to forgive sins, receive worship, and be one with God would be one of three options: insane, deceptive, or truly divine. Lewis wrote:

"You must make your choice. Either this man was, and is, the Son of God: or else a madman or something worse. You can shut Him up for a fool, you can spit at Him and kill Him as a demon; or you can fall at His feet and call Him Lord and God."[1]

Neutrality is not an option. Jesus claimed to be the Christ—the Son of the living God. That claim demands a response.

Today, some try to reduce Jesus to a moral philosopher, a spiritual guru, or a cultural revolutionary. But He will not be domesticated. His words and actions demand worship. Anything less is rejection.

The Evidence for Deity

Jesus accepted worship (Matthew 21:9; John 9:38), forgave sins (Mark 2:5–12), claimed eternal preexistence (John 8:58), and declared oneness with the Father (John 10:30). In doing so, He claimed what belongs only to God.

When He said, "Before Abraham was, I AM" (John 8:58), He took the divine name revealed in Exodus 3:14. The crowd understood—and picked up stones to kill Him.

John 1:1 declares, "In the beginning was the Word, and the Word was with God, and the Word was God." Verse 14 clarifies: "And the Word became flesh and dwelt among us."

Jesus Christ is not just a prophet, not just a rabbi, not just a miracle worker. He is God incarnate.

Further evidence includes the fulfillment of over 300 Old Testament prophecies, the miracles He performed—such as calming storms, raising the dead, and healing the sick—and the resurrection from the dead. These are not merely symbols; they are historical truths that anchor faith in reality.

The Crucial Confession

When Jesus stood trial before the high priest, He was asked directly, "Tell us if You are the Christ, the Son of God!" (Matthew 26:63). Jesus answered: "It is as you said" (v. 64). He affirmed His identity and sealed His fate.

He was mocked, beaten, and condemned—not for a crime, but for who He claimed to be. His confession cost Him His life—and purchased ours.

Peter's confession in Matthew 16:16—"You are the Christ, the Son of the living God"—was praised by Jesus as a revelation from the Father. Upon this confession, Jesus said He would build His church (Matthew 16:18).

The early church thrived on this truth. Stephen died proclaiming Christ. Paul preached Christ crucified. The apostles declared, "There is no other name under heaven given among men by which we must be saved" (Acts 4:12).

---

[1] C. S. Lewis, *The Complete C. S. Lewis Signature Classics* (New York: HarperCollins, 2002), 51." 1

What Will You Do with Jesus?

In John 12:42-43, many rulers believed in Jesus but would not confess Him. Why? "For they loved the praise of men more than the praise of God."

Today, many still believe intellectually that Jesus is the Christ—but they stop short of full allegiance. The true test is not just what we think of Christ—but what we will do with that belief.

Will we follow Him when it is costly? Will we obey Him when it is inconvenient? Will we confess Him openly, no matter the consequence?

Faith that does not confess is incomplete. Romans 10:9 declares, "If you confess with your mouth the Lord Jesus and believe in your heart that God has raised Him from the dead, you will be saved."

Confession leads to transformation. It means surrender. It means allegiance. It means placing Jesus above career, reputation, comfort, and even life itself.

Living Out the Confession

Confessing Christ is not a one-time event; it is a lifestyle. Every decision reflects what we think of Jesus. How we speak, how we serve, how we suffer—these all declare our theology.

- Do we serve others sacrificially, as Christ did?
- Do we forgive as we have been forgiven?
- Do we uphold truth even when it costs us?
- Do we love the unlovable?

A true confession transforms everything. It produces holiness, courage, compassion, and obedience. It moves us to action. It fuels our worship and shapes our mission.

Conclusion

The question *"What do you think of the Christ?"* is not just for Pharisees in the temple. It is for every soul today. Who is Jesus to you?

In the future, every knee will bow, and every tongue will confess that Jesus Christ is Lord (Philippians 2:10-11). Better to confess Him now—voluntarily, joyfully, courageously—than too late, at the judgment seat.

So, what do you think of the Christ?

Based on your belief, what will you do with Him today?

The answer to that question is not just a theological statement—it is the determining factor of your eternity.

Discussion Questions

1. Why did Jesus ask the religious leaders about the Christ's identity?
2. What does Psalm 110:1 reveal about Jesus?
3. Why is it insufficient to believe Jesus is only a good teacher?
4. How does John 1:1–14 support the divinity of Christ?
5. Why did Jesus' confession lead to His crucifixion?
6. What prevents people today from fully confessing Christ?
7. How does Jesus' identity shape your daily choices?
8. What does it mean to "confess" Christ in today's culture?
9. How would you respond if your faith were put to the test?
10. What does it look like to love the praise of God more than the praise of men?

Additional Verses

1. **Matthew 22:41–46** — "While the Pharisees were gathered together, Jesus asked them, saying, 'What do you think about the Christ? Whose Son is He?' They said to Him, 'The Son of David.' He said to them, 'How then does David in the Spirit call Him "Lord," saying: "The Lord said to my Lord, 'Sit at My right hand, till I make Your enemies Your footstool'"? If David then calls Him "Lord," how is He his Son?' And no one was able to answer Him a word, nor from that day on did anyone dare question Him anymore."

2. **Isaiah 9:6–7** — "Unto us a Child is born, unto us a Son is given; and the government will be upon His shoulder. And His name will be called Wonderful, Counselor, Mighty God, Everlasting Father, Prince of Peace. Of the increase of His government and peace there will be no end, upon the throne of David and over His kingdom, to order it and establish it with judgment and justice from that time forward, even forever. The zeal of the Lord of hosts will perform this."

3. **Psalm 110:1** — "The Lord said to my Lord, 'Sit at My right hand, till I make Your enemies Your footstool.'"

4. **John 1:14** — "The Word became flesh and dwelt among us, and we beheld His glory, the glory as of the only begotten of the Father, full of grace and truth."

5. **John 8:58** — "Jesus said to them, 'Most assuredly, I say to you, before Abraham was, I AM.'"

6. **Mark 2:5–12** — "When Jesus saw their faith, He said to the paralytic, 'Son, your sins are forgiven you.' And some of the scribes were sitting there and reasoning in their hearts, 'Why does this Man speak blasphemies like this? Who can forgive sins but God alone?' But immediately, when Jesus perceived in His spirit that they reasoned thus within themselves, He said to them, 'Why do you reason about these things in your hearts? Which is easier, to say to the paralytic, "Your sins are forgiven you," or to say, "Arise, take up your bed and walk"? But

that you may know that the Son of Man has power on earth to forgive sins'—He said to the paralytic, 'I say to you, arise, take up your bed, and go to your house.' Immediately he arose, took up the bed, and went out in the presence of them all, so that all were amazed and glorified God, saying, 'We never saw anything like this!'"

7. **John 10:30** — "I and My Father are one."

8. **Matthew 26:63–64** — "Jesus kept silent. And the high priest answered and said to Him, 'I put You under oath by the living God: Tell us if You are the Christ, the Son of God!' Jesus said to him, 'It is as you said. Nevertheless, I say to you, hereafter you will see the Son of Man sitting at the right hand of the Power, and coming on the clouds of heaven.'"

9. **John 12:42–43** — "Nevertheless even among the rulers many believed in Him, but because of the Pharisees they did not confess Him, lest they should be put out of the synagogue; for they loved the praise of men more than the praise of God."

10. **Philippians 2:9–11** — "Therefore God also has highly exalted Him and given Him the name which is above every name, that at the name of Jesus every knee should bow, of those in heaven, and of those on earth, and of those under the earth, and that every tongue should confess that Jesus Christ is Lord, to the glory of God the Father."

"Unto us a Child is born. . . . And His name will be called Wonderful, Counselor, Mighty God, Everlasting Father, Prince of Peace."

ISAIAH 9:6

POLISHING THE
PULPIT

02

By What Authority Do You Do These Things?

The Sovereignty of Christ Over All

Cliff Goodwin

"And they said to Him, 'By what authority are You doing these things? And who gave You this authority to do these things?'" —**MARK 11:28**

The Question of Authority

"By what authority?" That was the challenge hurled at Jesus by the chief priests, scribes, and elders in Mark 11. This was no casual inquiry. It was a hostile demand aimed at undermining Jesus' legitimacy. He had just cleansed the temple, taught the people, healed the blind and the lame, and received the praise of the masses. To the religious elite, His actions were offensive—especially because He acted without their approval. In effect, they were asking: *Who do You think You are?*

Jesus had entered their sacred space and turned it upside down—literally and spiritually. The temple, which had become a den of thieves, was reclaimed by its rightful Lord. And now they wanted answers.

But the deeper question is not about what Jesus thought of Himself. It is about what *we* think of Him. Do we recognize His authority? Do we bow before it? This question still challenges us today. When Jesus speaks—through His Word, through His church, through the Spirit's conviction—do we listen? Or do we ask, as they did, "By what authority?"

A Significant Event — The Resurrection of Christ

The authority of Jesus is most clearly and fully established by His resurrection. Matthew 28 begins with this victorious moment. An angel rolls the stone away. The guards tremble. The women rejoice. Jesus is alive!

Then He makes a bold declaration: "All authority has been given to Me in heaven and on earth" (Matthew 28:18). This was not just a claim—it was the aftermath of conquest. He had conquered sin, death, and the grave. Now, the crown was rightfully His.

Peter affirms this in Acts 2, where he preaches that God raised Jesus because "it was not possible that He should be held by it [death]" (Acts 2:24). Why? Because Scripture had prophesied His resurrection (Psalm 16:8–11). God's word cannot be broken (John 10:35), and so Jesus arose.

Paul echoes this in Romans 1:4, stating that Jesus was "declared to be the Son of God with power . . . by the resurrection from the dead." The empty tomb proves that Jesus is not just a teacher or prophet—He is the Son of God, the sovereign Lord of all.

The resurrection is God's stamp of approval on everything Jesus did and taught. It affirms His right to command, correct, and call all people to repentance. Without the resurrection, Christianity collapses; with it, Christ is enthroned.

A Significant Expression — "In Heaven and On Earth"

When Jesus says, "All authority has been given to Me in heaven and on earth," He is establishing the breadth of His reign. It is not partial, regional, or temporary. It is total, global, and eternal.

Authority in Heaven

In heaven, Jesus is exalted above the angels. Hebrews 1 makes this clear: "Having become so much better than the angels, as He has by inheritance obtained a more excellent name than they" (v. 4). The angels worship Him. All celestial beings are subject to Him (1 Peter 3:22).

Moreover, Colossians 1:20 tells us that His blood reconciles not only earthly things but "things in heaven." This likely refers to the faithful saints under the old covenant whose full redemption came through Christ's sacrifice. His blood flowed backward and forward in time, uniting all the faithful in one redemptive act.

In Revelation 5:12, heaven erupts in worship: "Worthy is the Lamb who was slain to receive power and riches and wisdom, and strength and honor and glory and blessing!" All of heaven bows before Jesus. His authority there is uncontested and eternal.

Authority on Earth

On earth, Jesus reigns supreme. Ephesians 1:22–23 states that God "put all things under His feet and gave Him to be head over all things to the church." His authority is not limited to spiritual matters; it encompasses the globe.

Wherever we stand—North America, Africa, Asia—we stand under Christ's authority. More specifically, His authority is fully realized in the church, His body. Colossians 1:18 says, "He is the head of the body, the church . . . that in all things He may have the preeminence."

His reign is not future only; it is present. He is Lord *now*. His word governs our lives, shapes our morals, directs our worship, and defines our mission. Jesus is not merely our Savior—He is our King.

A Significant Expectation — Submission to His Authority

To claim that Jesus has all authority is to affirm a truth that demands a response. If He reigns, we must submit.

This submission begins in worship. Colossians 3:16–17 calls us to sing "psalms and hymns and spiritual songs," letting the word of Christ dwell in us richly. Paul immediately follows with, "And whatever you do in word or deed, do all in the name of the Lord Jesus" (v. 17). Worship that is unauthorized is unacceptable.

This principle applies beyond worship. It governs our beliefs, our moral choices, our church practices, and even our speech. To do something "in the name of Jesus" is to do it by His authority.

Too often, religious practices drift from Scripture into tradition. Human inventions replace divine instructions. We must constantly ask, "By what authority do we do these things?" If the answer is not "By Christ's word," then we must repent.

Jesus challenged tradition in His own day: "Why do you also transgress the commandment of God because of your tradition?" (Matthew 15:3). He still asks that question today.

When the church holds fast to Scripture and rejects the traditions of men, it acknowledges Christ's headship. When it bows to human councils, creeds, or conferences, it denies His lordship.

A Significant Exception — The Father's Supremacy

Someone might ask, "If Jesus has all authority, does that mean He is above the Father?" No. Even here, Scripture gives clarity.

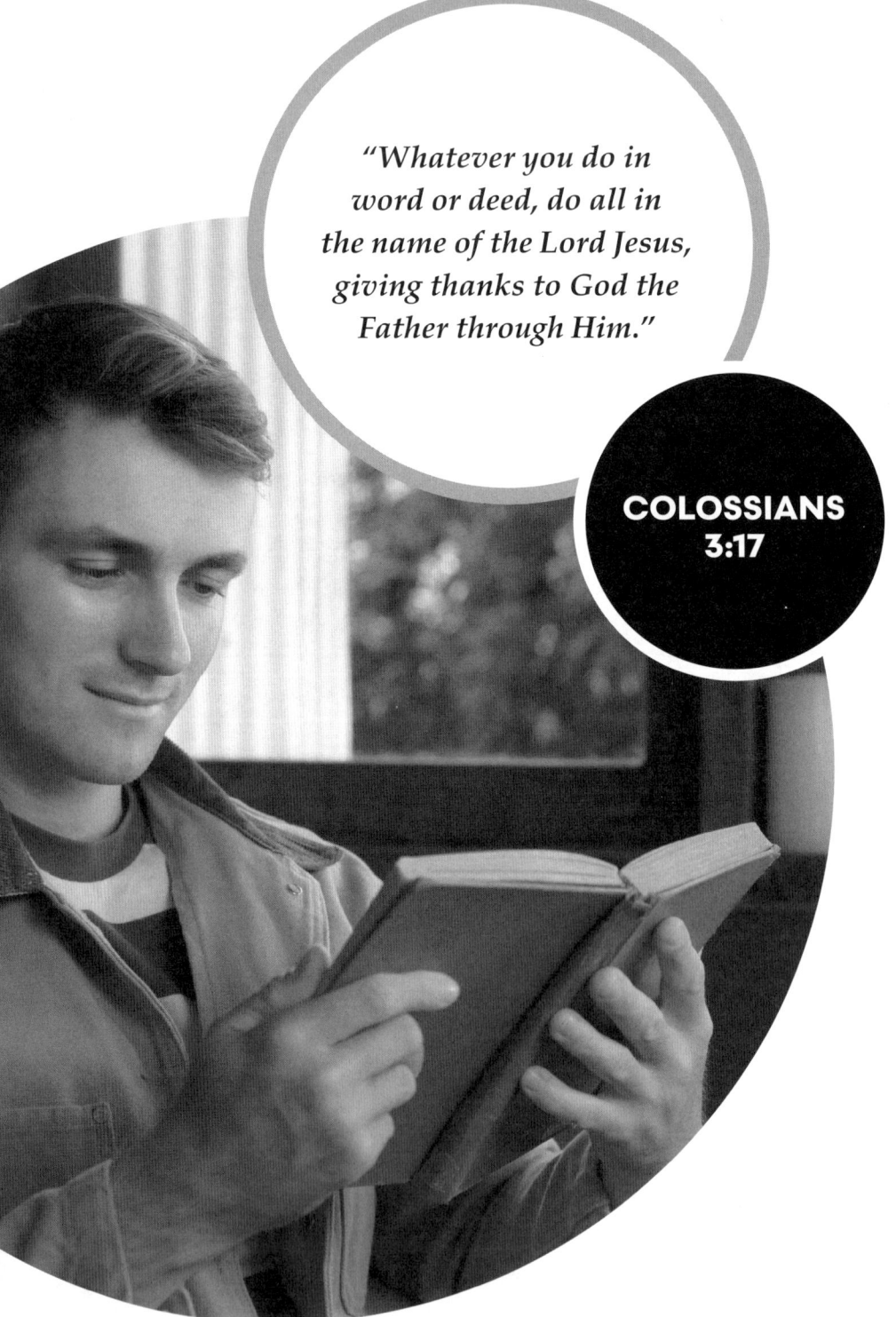

"Whatever you do in word or deed, do all in the name of the Lord Jesus, giving thanks to God the Father through Him."

COLOSSIANS 3:17

In 1 Corinthians 15:27, Paul says, "He has put all things under His feet." But then he adds, "It is evident that He who put all things under Him is excepted." The Father is the one exception. He gave the authority to the Son, and the Son will one day deliver the kingdom back to the Father (1 Corinthians 15:24).

This does not diminish Jesus—it defines the order within the Godhead. Jesus is fully divine, yet submissive to the Father's ultimate will. His authority is comprehensive, but it is derived. It was given.

Even during His earthly ministry, Jesus made this clear: "I do not seek My own will but the will of the Father who sent Me" (John 5:30). Obedience is not weakness—it is strength under submission.

This divine structure is reflected in the church and the home. Husbands and wives, elders and members, teachers and students—all must navigate roles that balance authority and submission in godly ways.

Conclusion: Who Do You Say That He Is?

The religious leaders asked, "By what authority do You do these things?" But the more important question is: *Do you acknowledge His authority?*

Jesus healed the sick, welcomed the praise of the people, taught with wisdom, and died in sacrifice. But He also arose in power, reigns in heaven, and will return in judgment.

Have you submitted to His authority? Have you placed your faith in Him (John 8:24)? Have you repented of your sins (2 Peter 3:9)? Have you confessed Him as Lord (Romans 10:9–10)? Have you been baptized to have your sins washed away (Acts 22:16)?

And if you once obeyed but have drifted, will you return? Will you surrender anew to His will?

The day is coming when every knee will bow, and every tongue will confess Jesus Christ as Lord (Philippians 2:10–11). Better to bow now in joyful surrender than to bow later in fearful judgment.

What will you say when Jesus asks, "By what authority do *you* live?" May your answer be, "By Yours, Lord—and Yours alone."

Discussion Questions

1. What actions of Jesus led to the question about His authority?
2. Why is the resurrection so central to Jesus' authority?
3. How does Jesus' authority in heaven differ from His authority on earth?
4. What does Colossians 1:20 teach about Christ's cosmic reconciliation?

5. How should recognizing Jesus' authority shape our worship practices?

6. Why is it dangerous to follow human traditions over Christ's commands?

7. How does the Father's "exception" in 1 Corinthians 15 help us understand the Godhead?

8. In what areas of your life is it most difficult to submit to Jesus' authority?

9. What does it mean to do "all in the name of the Lord Jesus" (Colossians 3:17)?

10. How can we grow in our daily surrender to Christ's lordship?

Additional Verses

1. **Mark 11:28** — "They said to Him, 'By what authority are You doing these things? And who gave You this authority to do these things?'"

2. **Matthew 28:18** — "Jesus came and spoke to them, saying, 'All authority has been given to Me in heaven and on earth.'"

3. **Acts 2:24** — "Whom God raised up, having loosed the pains of death, because it was not possible that He should be held by it."

4. **Romans 1:4** — "Declared to be the Son of God with power according to the Spirit of holiness, by the resurrection from the dead."

5. **Colossians 1:18** — "He is the head of the body, the church, who is the beginning, the firstborn from the dead, that in all things He may have the preeminence."

6. **1 Peter 3:22** — "[Jesus Christ,] who has gone into heaven and is at the right hand of God, angels and authorities and powers having been made subject to Him."

7. **Ephesians 1:22–23** — "He put all things under His feet, and gave Him to be head over all things to the church, which is His body, the fullness of Him who fills all in all."

8. **Hebrews 1:4** — "Having become so much better than the angels, as He has by inheritance obtained a more excellent name than they."

9. **1 Corinthians 15:27** — "'He has put all things under His feet.' But when He says 'all things are put under Him,' it is evident that He who put all things under Him is excepted."

10. **Colossians 3:17** — "Whatever you do in word or deed, do all in the name of the Lord Jesus, giving thanks to God the Father through Him."

03

What Do You Do More Than Others?

Imitating the Father Beyond the World's Standard

Eric Owens

"And if you greet your brethren only, what do you do more than others? Do not even the tax collectors do so?" —**MATTHEW 5:47**

The King Has Sat Down

Matthew's biography opens with an astounding proclamation: The King has arrived. With Jesus' birth, baptism, and temptation behind Him, His ministry begins. By the time we reach Matthew 5, the King has sat down, ready to teach, and not just to lecture—but to transform. He is Immanuel, God with us (Matthew 1:23), the Word made flesh (John 1:14), come to show us the way of the Father.

Among the most profound questions He asks is this: *What do you do more than others?* (Matthew 5:47).

Jesus is not measuring productivity or output. He is measuring character. He contrasts His disciples with the world. His question is meant to pierce us: If you love like the world loves, if you greet like the world greets, if you live like the world lives—what difference has following Jesus made?

The Correction of Love

Jesus begins this section by dismantling a common error: "You have heard that it was said, 'You shall love your neighbor and hate your enemy'" (v. 43). This was not God's command—but a corruption. Nowhere does the Old Testament command hatred of enemies. Instead, Proverbs 25:21 says, "If your enemy is hungry, give him bread to eat."

Jesus corrects the error: "But I say to you, love your enemies, bless those who curse you, do good to those who hate you, and pray for those who spitefully use you and persecute you" (Matthew 5:44). This is not ordinary love. This is divine love.

Why? "That you may be sons of your Father in heaven" (v. 45). The imitation of God's love is the defining trait of His children.

The Character of God's Love

Jesus draws from nature to illustrate God's impartial, generous love: "He makes His sun rise on the evil and on the good and sends rain on the just and on the unjust" (v. 45).

God loves by decision, not by merit. His love is proactive. It is not a reaction to worthiness, but a reflection of His character, and we are called to imitate it.

Romans 5:8 affirms this: "God demonstrates His own love toward us, in that while we were still sinners, Christ died for us." He loved His enemies. He prayed for His executioners (Luke 23:34). He died for the ungrateful and ungodly.

This kind of love is not optional—it is essential. The church that reflects the Father's love will shine as light in the world (Philippians 2:15). When Christians display selfless, sacrificial love, they put Christ on display.

The Comparison with the World

Jesus then delivers the heart of His question: *What do you do more than others?* He highlights the standards of tax collectors and Gentiles—outsiders and sinners—who naturally love those who love them and greet only their kin.

To love only our friends is to live without transformation. To greet only those we like is to remain unredeemed. If disciples of Christ are indistinguishable from the world, the gospel has not yet shaped us.

Jesus' question uncovers hypocrisy. Many claim faith but show no difference in their relationships, their conversations, or their generosity. But true discipleship changes us. It calls us higher.

Paul warned of this same issue in 2 Timothy 3:5: "Having a form of godliness but denying its power." There is no power in a faith that mimics the world.

The Charge to Be Perfect

Jesus concludes with this: "Therefore you shall be perfect, just as your Father in heaven is perfect" (Matthew 5:48).

The word "perfect" here (Greek *teleios*) means "mature, complete, full-grown." This is not sinless perfection, but godly completeness. It is the fulfillment of God's image in us (Genesis 1:26–27). It is the realization of our calling as His children.

To be perfect is to love fully, without favoritism. It is to mirror the Father's nature. As children resemble their parents, so disciples must resemble their Lord.

The Family Way

Jesus came to teach us the "family way." Isaiah 2 foretold it: "He will teach us His ways, and we shall walk in His paths" (v. 3). Jesus now delivers that very instruction.

To do more than others means:

- **Loving differently** (Matthew 5:43–44)
- **Praying differently** (Matthew 6:5–15)
- **Giving differently** (Matthew 6:1–4)
- **Judging righteously** (Matthew 7:1–5)
- **Forgiving completely** (Matthew 6:14–15)

The Sermon on the Mount is not a list of rules; it is a portrait of the King's family. It paints a picture of what kingdom citizens look like in contrast to the citizens of the world.

To walk as the family walks means living out our faith publicly and privately. It means treating strangers with the same care we show our friends. It means reconciling quickly, forgiving freely, and worshiping humbly. It means allowing the Spirit to cultivate a heart that responds with mercy, not malice.

Practical Application: Ten Ways to Do More

1. **Cultivate Godly Character** — Be poor in spirit, meek, merciful, pure in heart (Matthew 5:3–10). These are traits that Gentiles and tax collectors do not pursue.
2. **Live with Purpose** — Be the salt of the earth and the light of the world (Matthew 5:13–16). Influence the world rather than absorbing its values.
3. **Focus on Christ** — Seek His will, not your own. Make His mission your mission.
4. **Walk by Faith, Not Law** — Do not just avoid sin; pursue holiness of heart.
5. **Love Enemies** — This is the chief distinction. Anyone can love friends. Only God's children love enemies.

6. **Do Good in Secret** — Give and pray without fanfare (Matthew 6:1–6).
7. **Prioritize Eternal Treasures** — Store treasures in heaven (Matthew 6:19–21).
8. **Reject Worry** — Trust in God's provision (Matthew 6:25–34).
9. **Judge with Grace** — Be self-aware and merciful in discernment.
10. **Obey Jesus Fully** — Build on the rock by doing what He says (Matthew 7:24).

When these become our way of life, we do not just do more—we become more. We become like Christ.

Living as Light in a Dim World

One of the most powerful images Jesus uses for His disciples is light. "You are the light of the world," He declares in Matthew 5:14. Light stands out in darkness. It exposes. It attracts. It transforms.

To do more than others is to shine when others hide, to stand when others fall, to speak when others remain silent.

This includes:

- Speaking kindly when others gossip
- Remaining calm when others panic
- Showing grace when others retaliate
- Serving when others seek comfort

When we walk this way, the world notices, but not because we draw attention to ourselves. Instead, our lives point upward—to the Father.

As Jesus says: "Let your light so shine before men, that they may see your good works and glorify your Father in heaven" (Matthew 5:16).

Love Without Limits

God's love has no boundaries. It reaches across race, class, and history. To imitate this love means tearing down the walls that divide.

This might look like inviting the outsider to sit at your table. It might look like showing kindness to a coworker who mocks your faith. It may mean praying for someone who hurt you deeply.

Doing more than others means not settling for human standards of love and justice. It means reaching for divine ones.

Christ's Example and Expectation

Jesus lived what He preached. He did not merely tell us to love enemies—He demonstrated it. From the cross, He prayed for forgiveness for those who nailed Him there. He healed the servant of those who came to arrest Him. He dined with sinners, touched lepers, and wept over cities that rejected Him.

He calls us to walk the same path. "A new commandment I give to you, that you love one another; as I have loved you" (John 13:34).

To follow Jesus is not merely to believe in Him—it is to walk in His steps (1 Peter 2:21).

Conclusion

The question remains: *What do you do more than others?* Not in comparison to other Christians—but in contrast to a world that knows not God. Do you greet only your friends? Do you love only those who love you? Or have you taken up your cross to imitate the Father who loves the ungrateful and the wicked?

If your speech, your attitude, your love, and your priorities mirror the world's, then Jesus' question still echoes: *What difference has discipleship made?*

Let your answer be more than words. Let it be your walk.

Be different. Be holy. Be His.

Do more than others.

Discussion Questions

1. How does Jesus' teaching on love differ from the world's teaching?
2. Why is God's impartial love so important for Christians to imitate?
3. What are practical ways to love your enemies?
4. What does "doing more than others" look like in your daily life?
5. How can we guard against hypocrisy in love and service?
6. Why does Jesus link our love to our identity as God's children?
7. How does the Sermon on the Mount challenge your current lifestyle?
8. In what ways do you find it hardest to "do more than others"?
9. What does it mean to be "perfect" as our Father is perfect?
10. How can you reflect more of God's character this week?

Additional Verses

1. **Matthew 5:47** — "If you greet your brethren only, what do you do more than others? Do not even the tax collectors do so?"
2. **Matthew 5:44** — "I say to you, love your enemies, bless those who curse you, do good to those who hate you, and pray for those who spitefully use you and persecute you."

3. **Matthew 5:45** — "That you may be sons of your Father in heaven; for He makes His sun rise on the evil and on the good, and sends rain on the just and on the unjust."

4. **Matthew 5:48** — "Therefore you shall be perfect, just as your Father in heaven is perfect."

5. **Romans 5:8** — "God demonstrates His own love toward us, in that while we were still sinners, Christ died for us."

6. **Luke 23:34** — "Jesus said, 'Father, forgive them, for they do not know what they do.' And they divided His garments and cast lots."

7. **Proverbs 25:21** — "If your enemy is hungry, give him bread to eat; and if he is thirsty, give him water to drink."

8. **Isaiah 2:3** — "Many people shall come and say, 'Come, and let us go up to the mountain of the Lᴏʀᴅ, to the house of the God of Jacob; He will teach us His ways, and we shall walk in His paths.' For out of Zion shall go forth the law, and the word of the Lᴏʀᴅ from Jerusalem."

9. **John 1:14** — "The Word became flesh and dwelt among us, and we beheld His glory, the glory as of the only begotten of the Father, full of grace and truth."

10. **Colossians 3:14** — "Above all these things put on love, which is the bond of perfection."

"I say to you, love your enemies, bless those who curse you, do good to those who hate you, and pray for those who spitefully use you and persecute you."

MATTHEW 5:44

04

What Is the Kingdom of God Like?

Small Beginnings, Eternal Shelter

Wade Webster

"Then He said, 'What is the kingdom of God like? And to what shall I compare it? It is like a mustard seed, which a man took and put in his garden; and it grew and became a large tree, and the birds of the air nested in its branches.'" —**LUKE 13:18–19**

The Mustard Seed Question

Preaching sometimes feels like trying to turn a mountain into a molehill—or the other way around. In this case, one of Jesus' smallest parables delivers one of the kingdom's grandest truths. Jesus raises a mighty question with these seven words: *What is the kingdom of God like?* He answers with a mustard seed.

This question may seem small, even simple, but behind it lies the glory of God's eternal kingdom. Through it, Jesus gives a glimpse into something beyond comprehension—using something as ordinary as a seed. He challenges our ideas about significance and impact, reminding us that what may appear inconsequential to the world holds infinite value in God's hands.

This divine question resonates beyond its first audience, echoing in every generation. In the same way a tiny acorn can become a mighty oak, so the kingdom begins in miniature but ends in majesty.

The Nature of a Parable

Jesus often taught with parables, using earthly pictures to explain heavenly truths. The Greek word *parabole* means "to place alongside." Like a boat drawn up beside a dock, a parable places a visible story alongside an invisible truth. Jesus was a master of this method. Mark 4:34 tells us, "Without a parable He did not speak to them."

Parables both revealed and concealed. They clarified truth for seekers and clouded it from scoffers. In Matthew 13:13, Jesus explained, "Therefore I speak to them in parables, because seeing they do not see, and hearing they do not hear, nor do they understand."

Among Jesus' parables, many dealt with the kingdom of God. At least fifteen parables are kingdom parables. Matthew 13 alone contains seven. Jesus wanted His hearers to understand the nature, value, and growth of the kingdom. These parables act like spiritual soil tests—those who truly want the kingdom will dig deeper.

The Seed — Humble Beginnings

The mustard seed was easy for people in Palestine to picture proverbially. Jesus refers to it as the "smallest of all seeds," a common Jewish idiom to describe something minuscule. And yet, from this tiny seed grows something astounding. It becomes a plant tall enough for birds to rest in—a symbol of transformation.

This smallness reflects the church's beginning. Jesus, the founder, was born in a manger, not a palace. He grew up in Nazareth, a place of no reputation. His early followers were fishermen and tax collectors, unlearned and simple men. The initial audience? The poor, the sick, and the outcasts.

Jesus said, "Do not fear, little flock, for it is your Father's good pleasure to give you the kingdom" (Luke 12:32). Little flock indeed. Before Pentecost, 120 believers gathered. But that number was about to grow.

Just as a seed contains power hidden from the naked eye, so the gospel holds spiritual force. A single sermon in Acts 2 added three thousand souls. By Acts 4, the number had grown to five thousand. Despite persecution, imprisonment, and martyrdom, the church spread like fire. Even Saul of Tarsus, who tried to stamp it out, became its fiercest preacher.

Small things do not stay small in God's kingdom. A whispered prayer becomes a life turned around. A cup of cold water offered in Jesus' name is rewarded eternally. A tract placed in a mailbox can change a generation. The kingdom's beginnings are humble, but its trajectory is heavenly.

The Shrub — Unexpected Growth

Luke calls it a "tree." Botanically, the mustard plant was a shrub, but in context it grew taller than expected—up to twelve feet in Palestine. It became a tree by comparison. Kingdom growth often defies expectations.

Think of God's promises to Abraham. Childless and aging, he heard, "I will multiply your descendants as the stars of the heaven" (Genesis 22:17). Sand, stars, dust—every direction he looked, God gave a picture of unimaginable growth.

Daniel 2 speaks of a stone cut without hands that becomes a great mountain and fills the earth. Isaiah 2 envisions all nations flowing to the house of God. Jesus' mustard seed mirrors these prophecies. It starts small, but it grows to dominate.

This growth is often hidden. Like yeast in dough (Luke 13:20–21), the kingdom works quietly, subtly, until the whole is leavened. A fisherman tells his neighbor. A servant speaks to her master. A letter is passed from one house church to another. So the kingdom expands.

Even today, growth continues in unseen places. Underground churches thrive under persecution. Digital evangelism reaches hearts across closed borders. A single believer in a remote village becomes a light to hundreds. The mustard seed still grows.

The Shelter — Safety for the Soul

In the parable, the birds of the air find shelter in the mustard tree. The kingdom is not only expansive—it is protective. It is a home.

This reflects a pattern throughout Scripture. Noah found refuge in the ark while the world flooded. Rahab and her family were saved within her home by the scarlet cord. The Israelites were spared by the blood on their doorposts.

Today, the church is that refuge. Hebrews 6:18 says, "We might have strong consolation, who have fled for refuge to lay hold of the hope set before us." We are sheltered from the wrath to come. Sheltered from purposelessness. Sheltered from spiritual famine.

The kingdom offers a sense of belonging in a world plagued by isolation. In a culture where many are spiritually homeless, the church stands as a sanctuary. Within its walls are love, truth, grace, and accountability. The church is not a museum of saints but a hospital for sinners.

Jesus' kingdom is not like any earthly nation. Its power does not lie in gold or armies. It is built on sacrifice and sealed by blood. It offers peace for the restless, joy for the sorrowful, and eternity for the dying.

Zechariah's Reminder

Zechariah 4:10 says, "Who has despised the day of small things?" When the world sees insignificance, God sees potential. Jesus fed five thousand with a boy's lunch. God began His people with one aged man and his barren wife. And He launched His eternal kingdom with a carpenter from Nazareth and a group of fishermen.

Never underestimate what God can do with a mustard seed. What starts as a whisper becomes a song. What begins in private becomes a public movement. What seems irrelevant becomes essential. The kingdom of God is like that—alive, advancing, and unshakeable.

Conclusion

Jesus' question in Luke 13:18 opens our eyes to the mystery and majesty of the church. From a seed to a shrub to a shelter, the kingdom of God grows beyond what we could imagine. It began in obscurity but stands now as a refuge for millions.

What is the kingdom of God like? It is like a mustard seed. Its growth continues in you. Let it take root.

Discussion Questions

1. Why do you think Jesus used such a small seed to describe the kingdom?
2. What does the growth of the mustard seed teach us about the nature of spiritual growth?
3. How have you seen the church grow from humble beginnings in your own life?
4. What are modern examples of "mustard seed moments" in ministry?
5. How does this parable encourage patience and faith?
6. In what ways does the kingdom provide shelter for you?
7. Why is it important to not despise small beginnings in your walk with God?
8. How can Christians continue to plant "seeds" for the kingdom today?
9. What opposition did the early church face that mirrors today's challenges?
10. What promise in this parable gives you the most hope?

Additional Verses

1. **Luke 13:18–19** — "He said, 'What is the kingdom of God like? And to what shall I compare it? It is like a mustard seed, which a man took and put in his garden; and it grew and became a large tree, and the birds of the air nested in its branches.'"
2. **Luke 12:32** — "Do not fear, little flock, for it is your Father's good pleasure to give you the kingdom."
3. **Acts 2:41** — "Then those who gladly received his word were baptized; and that day about three thousand souls were added to them."

4. **Daniel 2:35** — "Then the iron, the clay, the bronze, the silver, and the gold were crushed together, and became like chaff from the summer threshing floors; the wind carried them away so that no trace of them was found. And the stone that struck the image became a great mountain and filled the whole earth."

5. **Isaiah 2:2** — "Now it shall come to pass in the latter days that the mountain of the Lord's house shall be established on the top of the mountains, and shall be exalted above the hills; and all nations shall flow to it."

6. **Zechariah 4:10** — "For who has despised the day of small things? For these seven rejoice to see the plumb line in the hand of Zerubbabel. They are the eyes of the Lord, which scan to and fro throughout the whole earth."

7. **Hebrews 6:18** — "That by two immutable things, in which it is impossible for God to lie, we might have strong consolation, who have fled for refuge to lay hold of the hope set before us."

8. **Genesis 22:17** — "Blessing I will bless you, and multiplying I will multiply your descendants as the stars of the heaven and as the sand which is on the seashore; and your descendants shall possess the gate of their enemies."

9. **Matthew 13:31–32** — "Another parable He put forth to them, saying: 'The kingdom of heaven is like a mustard seed, which a man took and sowed in his field, which indeed is the least of all the seeds; but when it is grown it is greater than the herbs and becomes a tree, so that the birds of the air come and nest in its branches.'"

10. **Luke 17:6** — "So the Lord said, 'If you have faith as a mustard seed, you can say to this mulberry tree, "Be pulled up by the roots and be planted in the sea," and it would obey you.'"

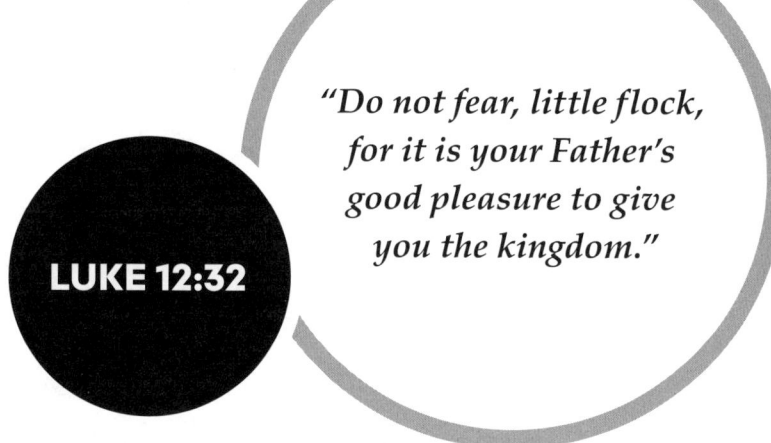

LUKE 12:32

"Do not fear, little flock, for it is your Father's good pleasure to give you the kingdom."

POLISHING THE
PULPIT

05

What Do You Seek?

*The First Question of Christ and
the Deepest Call to the Heart*

Greg Dismuke

"Then Jesus turned, and seeing them following, said to them, 'What do you seek?' They said to Him, 'Rabbi (which is to say, when translated, Teacher), where are You staying?' He said to them, 'Come and see.'" —**JOHN 1:38–39**

The First Question of Jesus

When Jesus began His public ministry, He did not begin with a command, a sermon, or a miracle. He began with a question. In John 1:38, His first recorded words are, "What do you seek?" It is not a question of location but of motivation. It is a question that cuts through all appearances and pierces the heart. It is a question every disciple must answer, then and now.

The disciples responded, "Rabbi, where are You staying?" And Jesus replied, "Come and see." This first exchange is pregnant with meaning. Their response was hesitant, perhaps unsure. Jesus did not lecture. He simply invited them to follow.

Today, this question still hangs in the air. What are you seeking? Why are you drawn to Jesus? Is it for comfort? For answers? For peace? For salvation? Or is it for something less enduring—riches, signs, or social belonging?

Seeking Christ for the Right Reason

Jesus' question demands honesty. Throughout His ministry, many sought Jesus—but not all sought Him for the right reasons. Some came to be fed (John 6:26). Others sought signs (Mark 8:12). Some, disturbingly, sought Him to trap Him or kill Him (John 8:37).

In John 6, after Jesus miraculously fed the five thousand, the crowd pursued Him across the sea. But He confronted them: "You seek Me, not because you saw the signs, but because you ate of the loaves and were filled" (John 6:26). They had missed the deeper significance. They wanted their bellies filled, not their souls.

Jesus warned them, "Do not labor for the food which perishes, but for the food which endures to everlasting life" (John 6:27). The same warning applies today. Many seek the temporal blessings of Christ but neglect the eternal life He offers.

What do you seek? Be honest.

The temptation to seek Jesus for selfish reasons has not gone away. Churches may swell with numbers when physical needs are being met but dwindle when spiritual truths challenge comfort zones. Following Jesus for the right reasons requires desire for truth, not just convenience. The faithful must examine their hearts regularly, remembering that Christ did not come merely to give bread, but to be the Bread of Life.

Testimonies of His Identity

If you are going to seek Jesus, you must know who He is. Fortunately, the testimony is abundant.

The Father's Testimony: At His baptism, a voice from heaven said, "This is My beloved Son, in whom I am well pleased" (Matthew 3:17). At the Transfiguration, the Father repeated the affirmation: "This is My beloved Son, in whom I am well pleased. Hear Him!" (Matthew 17:5).

John the Baptist's Testimony: John proclaimed, "Behold! The Lamb of God who takes away the sin of the world!" (John 1:29). He also testified that Jesus existed before him in divine nature, saying, "He who comes after me is preferred before me, for He was before me" (John 1:15).

The Apostle John's Testimony: "In the beginning was the Word, and the Word was with God, and the Word was God . . . and the Word became flesh and dwelt among us" (John 1:1, 14).

The Apostle Paul's Testimony: Paul declared Christ as "the image of the invisible God, the firstborn over all creation" (Colossians 1:15), and affirmed, "in Him dwells all the fullness of the Godhead bodily" (Colossians 2:9).

Even His Enemies Gave Testimony: When Jesus forgave the sins of the paralytic, His opponents reasoned, "Who can forgive sins but God alone?" (Mark 2:7). Their logic was correct. Jesus healed the man to prove He had divine authority: "That you may know that the Son of Man has power on earth to forgive sins" (Mark 2:10).

The Testimony of Miracles: Jesus' signs were not for show, but for proof. John 20:30–31 says, "Truly Jesus did many other signs . . . but these are written that you may believe that Jesus is the Christ, the Son of God." Each miracle is a confirmation.

Testimony abounds. The question is not whether Jesus is who He claims to be, but whether you will seek Him as He is.

What Are You Seeking?

The world today seeks Jesus for many reasons. Some noble. Some selfish. Some misguided.

- **The Material Seeker**: Like those in John 6, some seek Jesus as a provider of worldly blessings. They want financial gain, emotional comfort, or improved health. But Jesus warned against storing up treasures on earth (Matthew 6:19–21).
- **The Spectacle Seeker**: Others seek signs and wonders. They want the miraculous, the sensational, and the extraordinary. But Jesus sighed deeply at those who demanded a sign, saying that "no sign would be given to this generation" (Mark 8:11–12).
- **The Social Seeker**: Some seek Jesus for community. They enjoy the friendships, the potlucks, and the smiles. But when doctrine challenges their lifestyle, they fall away.
- **The Troubled Seeker**: Some come to Christ as a first-aid kit, an emergency resource in a time of crisis. They pray when life gets hard but vanish when storms subside.
- **The Academic Seeker**: Some pursue Jesus intellectually but resist transformation. They debate but never obey. Faith without surrender is ineffective.

True disciples seek Jesus because He is Lord. They seek Him for salvation, sanctification, and service. They seek to know Him and to be known by Him.

What You Will Find

To seek Christ rightly is to find more than you imagined.

- **The Reconciler** – "Yet now He has reconciled [you] in the body of His flesh through death" (Colossians 1:21–22).

- **The Justifier** — "Having now been justified by His blood, we shall be saved from wrath through Him" (Romans 5:9).
- **The Sanctifier** — "Sanctify them by Your truth. Your word is truth" (John 17:17).
- **The Savior** — "You shall call His name Jesus, for He will save His people from their sins" (Matthew 1:21).
- **The Healer** — "Those who are well have no need of a physician . . . I did not come to call the righteous, but sinners, to repentance" (Mark 2:17).
- **The Teacher** — "Rabbi, we know that You are a teacher come from God" (John 3:2).
- **The Redeemer** — "You were not redeemed with corruptible things . . . but with the precious blood of Christ" (1 Peter 1:18–19).
- **The High Priest** — "We have a great High Priest who has passed through the heavens" (Hebrews 4:14).
- **The Door** — "I am the door. If anyone enters by Me, he will be saved" (John 10:9).
- **The Light** — "I am the light of the world. He who follows Me shall not walk in darkness" (John 8:12).

Jesus satisfies every need of the soul. Seek Him, and you will not walk in darkness. Seek Him, and you will find rest for your soul (Matthew 11:28–30).

How to Seek Him

Jesus said, "Seek first the kingdom of God and His righteousness" (Matthew 6:33). He told those who asked about salvation, "Strive to enter through the narrow gate" (Luke 13:24). And through Paul, we learn that God "commands all men everywhere to repent" (Acts 17:30).

To seek Jesus rightly, you must

1. **Seek in the Right Manner** — Through the gospel, not mystical experience. "He called you by our gospel" (2 Thessalonians 2:14).
2. **Seek at the Right Moment** — "Behold, now is the accepted time" (2 Corinthians 6:2). Do not delay.
3. **Seek with the Right Meaning** — Seek not for benefits, but because you are dead in sins and need new life (Romans 6:3–4).
4. **Seek with Total Commitment** — "You shall love the Lord your God with all your heart, with all your soul, with all your mind, and with all your strength" (Mark 12:30). Halfhearted seekers rarely find Him.
5. **Seek in Humility** — "But on this one will I look: on him who is poor and of a contrite spirit" (Isaiah 66:2).

Jesus promised, "Ask, and it will be given to you; seek, and you will find; knock, and it will be opened to you" (Matthew 7:7). But the promise is for the earnest, not the apathetic.

The Ongoing Pursuit

Seeking Christ is not a one-time decision—it is a lifelong journey. Paul, near the end of his life, wrote, "That I may know Him and the power of His resurrection . . . I press toward the goal for the prize of the upward call of God in Christ Jesus" (Philippians 3:10–14).

Discipleship is a pursuit. We grow in grace, deepen in faith, and become more like Him through intentional effort. We must

- Study His Word diligently (2 Timothy 2:15).
- Walk in the Spirit daily (Galatians 5:16).
- Bear much fruit (John 15:5).
- Endure hardship as good soldiers (2 Timothy 2:3).

The Christian life is not passive. It is active, intentional, and focused on the author and finisher of our faith (Hebrews 12:1–2).

Conclusion

Jesus' first question is still His most pressing: *"What do you seek?"* It is a question that confronts your motives and clarifies your heart. If you are truly seeking Christ—not for miracles or material blessings, but for mercy, righteousness, and eternal life—then His invitation is the same: "Come and see."

What you find will change everything.

To seek Jesus is to find truth. To find truth is to find life. To find life is to find the One who makes all things new.

Let us not delay. Let us seek Him while He may be found (Isaiah 55:6). Let us follow wherever He leads.

Discussion Questions

1. What are some wrong motivations for seeking Jesus today?
2. How can we know if we are truly seeking Jesus for the right reasons?
3. Why do you think Jesus began His ministry with a question instead of a command?
4. What does it mean to labor for "the food which endures to everlasting life"? (John 6:27).
5. How do the testimonies about Jesus strengthen your faith?
6. Why do some people walk away from Jesus even after initially following Him?
7. What comfort does it bring to know that Jesus is our High Priest and Advocate?
8. What is the danger of delaying your response to the gospel?
9. How does seeking Jesus change your priorities and desires?
10. In what ways can we help others seek Jesus for who He truly is?

Additional Verses

1. **John 1:38** — "Jesus turned, and seeing them following, said to them, 'What do you seek?'"

2. **John 6:26** — "Jesus answered them and said, 'Most assuredly, I say to you, you seek Me, not because you saw the signs, but because you ate of the loaves and were filled.'"

3. **Matthew 3:17** — "Suddenly a voice came from heaven, saying, 'This is My beloved Son, in whom I am well pleased.'"

4. **Colossians 1:15** — "He is the image of the invisible God, the firstborn over all creation."

5. **Mark 2:10** — "The Son of Man has power on earth to forgive sins."

6. **Matthew 6:33** — "Seek first the kingdom of God and His righteousness, and all these things shall be added to you."

7. **Acts 17:30** — "Truly, these times of ignorance God overlooked, but now commands all men everywhere to repent."

8. **2 Corinthians 6:2** — "He says: 'In an acceptable time I have heard you, and in the day of salvation I have helped you.' Behold, now is the accepted time; behold, now is the day of salvation."

9. **John 10:9** — "I am the door. If anyone enters by Me, he will be saved, and will go in and out and find pasture."

10. **Hebrews 4:14** — "Seeing then that we have a great High Priest who has passed through the heavens, Jesus the Son of God, let us hold fast our confession."

MATTHEW 11:28

"Come to Me, all you who labor and are heavy laden, and I will give you rest."

06

What Will It Profit?

An Examination of Mark 8:36–37

Don Blackwell

"For what will it profit a man if he gains the whole world, and loses his own soul? Or what will a man give in exchange for his soul?" — **MARK 8:36**

A Tragic Trade

The world is full of stories of people who made tragic trades. Consider the recent media storm about a high-powered CEO caught in a scandalous affair. The headlines read like modern-day parables: A man trades his marriage, his family, and his career for a fleeting moment of pleasure. It is easy to look at such decisions and shake our heads, but Jesus compels us to ask a deeper question: *Would I ever make that trade?*

In Mark 8:36–37, Jesus forces every person to weigh his or her life on eternal scales. This is not a rhetorical question—it is a call for soul-level evaluation. In this passage, we find four movements: Evaluation, Expiration, Explanation, and Invitation.

Evaluation: The Soul Vs. the World

Jesus begins by placing two things side by side: the soul and the whole world. He asks, "What will it profit a man if he gains the whole world, and loses his own soul?" The "world" in this context includes the pleasures, possessions, prestige, and power that lure men away from God.

John wrote, "Do not love the world or the things in the world . . . the lust of the flesh, the lust of the eyes, and the pride of life" (1 John 2:15–16). Let us consider a few tragic trades people make.

Money

Some people trade their souls for wealth. The rich young ruler is a classic example. Jesus told him to sell all he had and follow Him. Unfortunately, "when the young man heard that saying, he went away sorrowful, for he had great possessions" (Matthew 19:22).

Money appeals to all three lusts: the flesh (comfort), the eyes (coveting), and pride (status). Many people who focus on money, including Christians, drift into destruction without even realizing it (1 Timothy 6:10; Luke 8:14).

Popularity

Ananias and Sapphira craved admiration, so they lied (Acts 5). Religious leaders in John 12 believed in Jesus but remained silent to avoid losing status, "for they loved the praise of men more than the praise of God" (John 12:43).

Pilate also traded truth for approval. "Wishing to gratify the crowd, he released Barabbas" (Mark 15:15). Today, whether teenagers seek peer approval or professionals seek acceptance in worldly circles, many have sold their souls just to be liked.

Relationships

A man once allowed his wife to die in their unscriptural marriage rather than lead her in repentance. Through tears, he admitted, "I let my wife die lost." It haunted him until his own death. Jesus must be loved above even family (Matthew 10:37). No human relationship is worth your eternal soul.

Pleasure

Paul warned about Demas, who "loved this present world" (2 Timothy 4:10). Not all pleasure is sinful, but it becomes damning when it replaces the purpose of life. "She who lives in pleasure is dead while she lives" (1 Timothy 5:6). The rich fool in Luke 12 had wealth, leisure, and plans; God called him a fool because he forgot his soul.

Neglect

Some do not lose their souls through scandal, but through silence. They simply never serve. Paul emphasized the importance of "always abounding in the work of the Lord" (1 Corinthians 15:58) and being "zealous for good works" (Titus 2:14). Many Christians are spiritually perishing not because of evil choices, but because of empty calendars.

The Bottom Line

It is not just one trade Jesus asks us to consider—it is *the whole world*. If you gained everything—every dollar, every like, every thrill—would it be worth your soul?

"If anyone loves the world, the love of the Father is not in him. For all that is in the world—the lust of the flesh, the lust of the eyes, and the pride of life—is not of the Father but is of the world. And the world is passing away, and the lust of it; but he who does the will of God abides forever."

1 JOHN 2:15–17

Expiration: Deny Yourself (Mark 8:34)

"Expiration" here does not mean spoilage—it means death. Denial of self is not optional. Jesus calls us to put to death the worldly desires that war against our souls. "Whoever desires to come after Me, let him deny himself, and take up his cross, and follow Me" (Mark 8:34).

Taking up your cross is not about bearing life's inconveniences. In the first century, a man who took up his cross was walking to his execution. Jesus is asking us to die to ourselves—to crucify our pride, passions, and personal preferences. "I have been crucified with Christ; it is no longer I who live, but Christ lives in me" (Galatians 2:20).

Explanation: Lose to Save (Mark 8:35)

"For whoever desires to save his life will lose it, but whoever loses his life for My sake and the gospel's will save it" (Mark 8:35). The paradox is simple: to gain eternal life, you must give up this temporary life. Paul understood this well: "But what things were gain to me, these I have counted loss for Christ . . . and count them as rubbish, that I may gain Christ" (Philippians 3:7–8).

Jesus is not calling you to literal death, but to a life of sacrifice. You may not lose your physical body, but you will lose worldly dreams. In return, you will gain life that never ends.

Invitation: Who Will Come?

In Mark 8, notice how Jesus called people in general, including His disciples. He said, "Whoever desires to come after Me . . ." (Mark 8:34), and "Whoever loses his life for My sake . . ." (Mark 8:35).

This invitation is open to all. There is no predetermination, no favoritism. Jesus says "whoever"—that means you. However, notice also the word "desires." God will not force you. You must *want* to come. You must *choose* to follow. You must *decide* that your soul is more valuable than this world. Jesus does not promise comfort. He promises a cross—but He also promises a crown.

Why Is Your Soul So Valuable?

First, your soul is valuable because you are made in the image of God. In the beginning, God said, "Let Us make man in Our image" (Genesis 1:26), and the New Testament reinforces that statement as well: "We are His offspring" (Acts 17:28).

Second, your soul was purchased with Christ's blood. "You were not redeemed with silver or gold, but with the precious blood of Christ" (1 Peter 1:18–19). "While we were still sinners, Christ died for us" (Romans 5:8). Third, your soul is eternal in nature. Your body may last 70–80 years, but your soul lasts forever. Hell is eternal (Revelation 14:11; Mark 9:45). Heaven is eternal (Matthew 25:46).

A Final Illustration: Would You Trade It?

This author, Don Blackwell, is part of a study that may restore limited mobility through a neural implant. If it works, he would trade nearly anything—money, property, even time—to stand and walk again—but he would not trade his soul.

Why? Because no matter what he might gain or how much this world offers, he would not trade it for eternity.

"Have you counted the cost if your soul should be lost?"

Conclusion

Jesus' question is not theoretical. It is personal. It is eternal. "What will it profit a man if he gains the whole world, and loses his own soul?" You must answer; you must decide; you must choose now—before your opportunity expires.

Will you take up your cross and follow Him?
Will you make the only trade that truly profits—the soul for the Savior?

Discussion Questions

1. What are some modern ways people trade their souls?
2. Why do you think Jesus framed this issue as an exchange?
3. What makes the soul more valuable than the whole world?
4. How can pleasure or popularity become spiritual dangers?
5. What does "deny yourself and take up your cross" mean practically?
6. In what areas of life are you tempted to make a bad trade?
7. What steps can we take to keep our souls safe?
8. Why do you think some people drift rather than decide to leave God?
9. What role does eternity play in shaping daily decisions?
10. How can we help others see the true value of their souls?

Additional Verses

1. **Mark 8:36** — "What will it profit a man if he gains the whole world, and loses his own soul?"

2. **1 John 2:15–16** — "Do not love the world or the things in the world. If anyone loves the world, the love of the Father is not in him. For all that is in the world—the lust of the flesh, the lust of the eyes, and the pride of life—is not of the Father but is of the world."

3. **Genesis 1:26** — "God said, 'Let Us make man in Our image, according to Our likeness; let them have dominion over the fish of the sea, over the birds of the air,

and over the cattle, over all the earth and over every creeping thing that creeps on the earth.'"

4. **1 Peter 1:18–19** — "Knowing that you were not redeemed with corruptible things, like silver or gold, from your aimless conduct received by tradition from your fathers, but with the precious blood of Christ, as of a lamb without blemish and without spot."

5. **Matthew 10:28** — "Do not fear those who kill the body but cannot kill the soul. But rather fear Him who is able to destroy both soul and body in hell."

6. **1 Timothy 6:10** — "The love of money is a root of all kinds of evil, for which some have strayed from the faith in their greediness, and pierced themselves through with many sorrows."

7. **2 Timothy 4:10** — "Demas has forsaken me, having loved this present world, and has departed for Thessalonica—Crescens for Galatia, Titus for Dalmatia."

8. **Luke 12:19–20** — "I will say to my soul, 'Soul, you have many goods laid up for many years; take your ease; eat, drink, and be merry.' But God said to him, 'Fool! This night your soul will be required of you; then whose will those things be which you have provided?'"

9. **Galatians 2:20** — "I have been crucified with Christ; it is no longer I who live, but Christ lives in me; and the life which I now live in the flesh I live by faith in the Son of God, who loved me and gave Himself for me."

10. **Romans 8:18** — "For I consider that the sufferings of this present time are not worthy to be compared with the glory which shall be revealed in us."

MARK 8:35

"Whoever desires to save his life will lose it, but whoever loses his life for My sake and the gospel's will save it."

POLISHING THE PULPIT

Will He Find Faith?

The Final Question of Enduring Belief

Dan Winkler

"Nevertheless, when the Son of Man comes, will He really find faith on the earth?"

— **LUKE 18:8**

The Certainty of His Coming

Jesus' words begin with a certainty: *"When the Son of Man comes . . . ."* This is not speculation—it is a declaration of divine certainty. The Lord will return. This coming is as sure as His first. Scripture is saturated with the promise of His second coming: "This same Jesus, who was taken up from you into heaven, will so come in like manner" (Acts 1:11).

Jesus will not come in secret or silence. Matthew 25:31 says, "When the Son of Man comes in His glory, and all the holy angels with Him, then He will sit on the throne of His glory." His return will be visible, majestic, and world-altering.

Also, His return will be a moment of separation. The sheep will be divided from the goats (Matthew 25:32). The faithful will be welcomed: "Come, you blessed of My Father, inherit the kingdom prepared for you from the foundation of the world" (Matthew 25:34). The faithless will be dismissed: "Depart from Me, you cursed, into the everlasting fire" (Matthew 25:41).

The real question is not whether Christ will come again—but what He will find when He does. Specifically, will He find faith?

41

The Question of Faith

"Will He really find faith on the earth?" This question is not about religion in general. It is not asking whether churches will exist, whether people will claim to be spiritual, or whether religious ceremonies will be performed. It is asking about *true faith*—the kind that perseveres, obeys, trusts, and endures.

Jesus had just finished telling the parable of the persistent widow (Luke 18:1–7), teaching that we must always pray and not lose heart. The question that follows shows why this parable matters: *Enduring faith is rare.* It is one thing to believe when things are easy; it is another to persevere when prayers go unanswered and life grows dark.

Faith that endures through delay, doubt, and difficulty—that is what Jesus is looking for.

An Illustrative Scene: The Paralytic and the Scribes (Matthew 9:1–8)

This question of enduring, visible faith is vividly illustrated in Matthew 9. Jesus returns to His own city. A paralytic is brought to Him by friends, and Scripture says, "When Jesus saw their faith . . ." (v. 2). Not just their effort. Not just their desperation. Their *faith.*

The word used here implies something that can be seen—not just internal, but externally visible through action. Their faith tore through roofs, crossed obstacles, and refused to be turned away.

By contrast, the scribes standing nearby questioned Jesus' authority. They accused Him of blasphemy in their hearts. Jesus, knowing their thoughts, asked, "Why do you think evil in your hearts?" (v. 4). Two groups, two hearts: one faithful, one skeptical.

Faith is not merely mental assent. It is demonstrated in action. These friends had faith that moved them to carry, climb, and break through. The scribes had skepticism that left them immobile and critical.

What does Jesus see when He looks at your faith—movement or murmuring?

Types of Faith in the Gospel of Matthew

Throughout Matthew's Gospel, we are introduced to different kinds of faith. Jesus interacts with people of great faith, little faith, and even those who completely lack faith. Each encounter teaches us about the kind of faith that endures.

1. Great Faith (*Tosautēs*)

- **The Centurion (Matthew 8:10)** — A Roman soldier who asked Jesus to heal his servant from afar. Jesus marveled, "I have not found such great faith, not even in Israel!"
- **The Syrophoenician Woman (Matthew 15:28)** — A Gentile mother pleading for her daughter's healing. Jesus tested her, but she persisted. He answered, "O woman, great is your faith! Let it be to you as you desire."

What do these examples have in common? They are both Gentiles. Outsiders. Yet they trusted deeply in Jesus' power and mercy. Great faith recognizes authority and acts in humility.

2. Little Faith (*Oligopistoi*)

- **Worry (Matthew 6:30)** — Jesus said, "O you of little faith" when addressing anxious hearts. Faith trusts in God's provision.
- **Fear (Matthew 8:26)** — When the disciples panicked in the storm, Jesus asked, "Why are you fearful, O you of little faith?" Faith always believes, even in chaos.
- **Doubt (Matthew 14:31)** — When Peter began to sink after walking on water, Jesus said, "O you of little faith, why did you doubt?" Faith stays focused on Jesus.
- **Reasoning (Matthew 16:8)** — The disciples misunderstood His warning about the leaven of the Pharisees. Jesus said, "O you of little faith, why do you reason among yourselves?" Faith listens and learns.

Little faith is often distracted or discouraged. It still believes, but it wavers. Jesus corrects it—not to condemn, but to cultivate stronger faith.

3. Your Faith: Personalized Faith

Jesus often tied healing or blessing to an individual's personal faith:

- **Matthew 9:22** — "Your faith has made you well."
- **Matthew 9:29** — "According to your faith let it be to you."
- **Matthew 15:28** — "Great is your faith."

Faith is not inherited. It cannot be borrowed. It must be personal, cultivated, and active.

Faith and Affliction: Endurance in the Fire

Trials test faith. James wrote, "The testing of your faith produces patience" (James 1:3). Paul said, "We walk by faith, not by sight" (2 Corinthians 5:7). Faith is forged in fire.

When we are sick—will we pray like Jairus (Matthew 9:18)?

When we are disappointed—will we press on like the blind men (Matthew 9:27–30)?

When our prayers seem unanswered—will we persist like the Canaanite woman (Matthew 15:22–28)?

Jesus looks for faith that endures disappointment. He listens to the voice that keeps calling even when the door seems shut. He honors the heart that believes even in silence.

Faith is not the absence of pain—it is belief in spite of it.

Pharisee Mindset vs. Faith-Filled Heart (Matthew 23)

The scribes and Pharisees serve as a stark warning of religious appearance without true faith. In Matthew 23, Jesus exposes their hearts:

1. **They were prideful** — "They love the best places at feasts" (v. 6).
2. **They were hypocritical** — "They say, and do not do" (v. 3).
3. **They were superficial** — "You cleanse the outside . . . but inside they are full of extortion" (v. 25).
4. **They neglected the heart** — "You also outwardly appear righteous . . . but inside are full of hypocrisy" (v. 28).
5. **They focused on appearances** — "Their works they do to be seen of men. They make their phylacteries broad" (v. 5).
6. **They were blind guides** — Missing the heart of God's law (v. 24).

Their religious activity masked a lack of faith. Jesus lamented, "You are like whitewashed tombs" (v. 27).

Faith is not religious ritual. It is relationship. It is trust. It is surrender.

Self-Examination: Is There Faith in You?

Jesus' question must be internalized: *When He returns, will He find faith in me?*

- Does He see faith when I am suffering?
- Does He see faith when I am waiting?
- Does He see faith when I am praying?
- Does He see faith when I face temptation?
- Does He see faith when I am discouraged?

Faith is not measured by emotion, but by endurance. It clings to Christ through every storm, every loss, every silence.

Faith Until the End

Jesus told His disciples, "He who endures to the end shall be saved" (Matthew 24:13). The Christian life is not a sprint—it is a marathon. We are called to keep the faith, finish the race, and receive the crown (2 Timothy 4:7–8).

- Faith worships even when it costs (Hebrews 11:4).
- Faith walks with God when the world mocks (Hebrews 11:5).

- Faith builds the ark before the rain falls (Hebrews 11:7).
- Faith leaves comfort for calling (Hebrews 11:8).
- Faith waits patiently, sees the invisible, and welcomes the promises from afar (Hebrews 11:13).

These are the examples Jesus will be looking for when He comes. May He find them in us.

Discussion Questions

1. What is the difference between great faith and little faith?
2. Why does Jesus connect worry and fear to weak faith?
3. How can you cultivate a stronger faith during affliction?
4. What does Matthew 9:1–8 teach us about visible faith?
5. How did the Pharisees' reasoning differ from the paralytic's faith?
6. Which traits of the Pharisee mindset do you struggle with?
7. What areas of your life challenge your faith the most?
8. How can we resist the temptation to "major on minors"?
9. What does it mean to have enduring faith until Christ's return?
10. How would your faith look under Christ's inspection today?

Additional Verses

1. **Luke 18:8** — "When the Son of Man comes, will He really find faith on the earth?"

2. **Matthew 25:31–32** — "When the Son of Man comes in His glory, and all the holy angels with Him, then He will sit on the throne of His glory. All the nations will be gathered before Him, and He will separate them one from another, as a shepherd divides his sheep from the goats."

3. **Matthew 9:1–8** — "So He got into a boat, crossed over, and came to His own city. Then behold, they brought to Him a paralytic lying on a bed. When Jesus saw their faith, He said to the paralytic, 'Son, be of good cheer; your sins are forgiven you.' And at once some of the scribes said within themselves, 'This Man blasphemes!' But Jesus, knowing their thoughts, said, 'Why do you think evil in your hearts? For which is easier, to say, "Your sins are forgiven you," or to say, "Arise and walk"? But that you may know that the Son of Man has power on earth to forgive sins'—then He said to the paralytic, 'Arise, take up your bed, and go to your house.' And he arose and departed to his house. Now when the multitudes saw it, they marveled and glorified God, who had given such power to men."

4. **Matthew 8:10** — "When Jesus heard it, He marveled, and said to those who followed, 'Assuredly, I say to you, I have not found such great faith, not even in Israel!'"

5. **Matthew 15:28** — "Jesus answered and said to her, 'O woman, great is your faith! Let it be to you as you desire.' And her daughter was healed from that very hour."

6. **Matthew 6:30** — "Now if God so clothes the grass of the field, which today is, and tomorrow is thrown into the oven, will He not much more clothe you, O you of little faith?"

7. **Matthew 8:26** — "He said to them, 'Why are you fearful, O you of little faith?' Then He arose and rebuked the winds and the sea, and there was a great calm."

8. **Matthew 14:31** — "Immediately Jesus stretched out His hand and caught him, and said to him, 'O you of little faith, why did you doubt?'"

9. **Matthew 16:8** — "Jesus, being aware of it, said to them, 'O you of little faith, why do you reason among yourselves because you have brought no bread?'"

10. **Matthew 23:27–28** — "Woe to you, scribes and Pharisees, hypocrites! For you are like whitewashed tombs which indeed appear beautiful outwardly, but inside are full of dead men's bones and all uncleanness. Even so you also outwardly appear righteous to men, but inside you are full of hypocrisy and lawlessness."

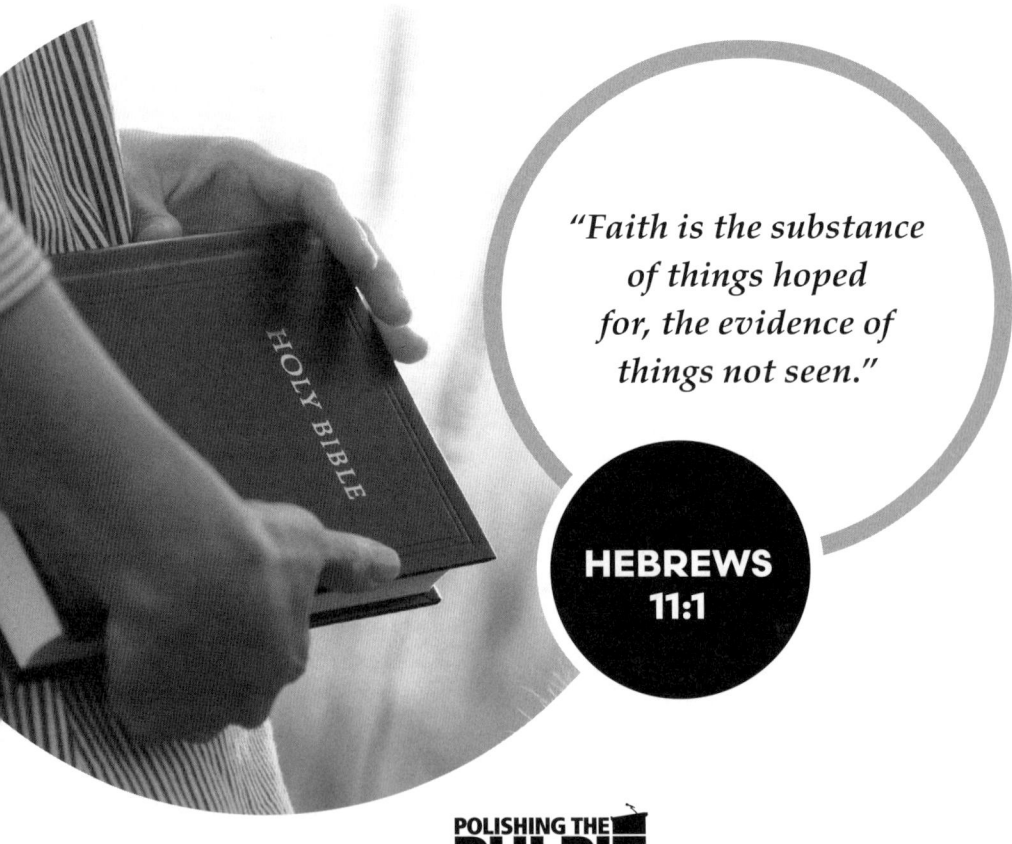

"*Faith is the substance of things hoped for, the evidence of things not seen.*"

HEBREWS 11:1

POLISHING THE PULPIT

Where Are the Nine?

The Faith That Returns to Give Thanks

Joe Wells

"So Jesus answered and said, 'Were there not ten cleansed? But where are the nine?'"

— LUKE 17:17

Ingratitude in an Age of Abundance

We live in an age of abundance and entitlement, yet gratitude seems increasingly rare. In Luke 17, Jesus heals ten lepers—but only one returns. Jesus asks a startling question: *"Where are the nine?"* These words cut deep into the human heart and reveal a fundamental trait of true discipleship: returning to give thanks.

The text is not merely a story about healing. It is a spiritual x-ray of the heart. It shows the difference between receiving blessings and responding to the Blesser; it forces us to ask, "Am I like the one—or the nine?"

The Setting: Between Samaria and Galilee

Jesus was passing between Samaria and Galilee—a border region between Jews and Samaritans. Historically hostile, these two groups rarely mixed. But leprosy, the great equalizer, bound them together in suffering.

Ten men stood at a distance, obeying Levitical law (Leviticus 13:45–46). They were united in pain and exile. In this place of isolation, they cried out, "Jesus, Master, have mercy on us!" (Luke 17:13).

The word "Master" here is significant. It is not the generic *kurios* (Lord) used by crowds. It is *epistata*—used only in Luke and always by disciples. This term recognizes authority, power, and position. These lepers were not casual bystanders; they addressed Jesus with reverence.

The Command: Go Show Yourselves to the Priests

Jesus responded, "Go, show yourselves to the priests" (Luke 17:14). According to the law (Leviticus 14), only a priest could declare a leper clean and restore him to community life. The text notes that "as they went, they were cleansed."

Their healing was conditional upon obedience. They were not healed before— they were healed *while* going. This shows a critical faith principle: Obedience often precedes the blessing. Faith walks even before sight sees.

One Turned Back

One of the ten, seeing that he had been healed, "returned, and with a loud voice glorified God, and fell down on his face at His feet, giving Him thanks. And he was a Samaritan" (Luke 17:15–16). Jesus' response is both observational and confrontational:

"Were there not ten cleansed? But where are the nine?" (v. 17)

He then commends the one who returned: "Your faith has made you well." The Greek word used (*sozo*) carries the idea of being saved, not just healed. The nine were cleansed; the one was made whole.

The Difference Between Being Healed and Being Whole

This distinction matters. All ten received healing, but only one received salvation. He returned not just to be thankful, but to worship. His heart responded to Jesus, not just His power.

This story shows us:

- **Faith initiates obedience** (they went).
- **Gratitude brings us back to Jesus** (he returned).
- **Worship reveals spiritual depth** (he fell at His feet).

Where Were the Nine?

Jesus asks, *"Where are the nine?"* He is not seeking GPS coordinates. He is revealing a contrast: The one who glorifies versus the many who consume and walk away.

Many today are content to receive God's blessings but never build a relationship. They want healing without holiness, help without humility. They want the gift—but not the Giver.

This question should pierce our own hearts: When was the last time we returned—not for more, but to give thanks?

The Samaritan Surprise

It is no small detail that the one who returned was a Samaritan. Jews considered Samaritans unclean, impure, and beyond spiritual fellowship. Yet Jesus highlights the man's gratitude and faith.

God often finds praiseworthy qualities in unexpected places. Luke 13:30 says, "Indeed there are last who will be first, and there are first who will be last."

This echoes the parable of the Good Samaritan (Luke 10). Jesus frequently shows that outsiders can be examples of spiritual insight and love.

Faith and Gratitude Must Go Together

Faith that does not result in gratitude is incomplete. The nine had enough faith to walk to the priests but not enough to return to the feet of Jesus.

Gratitude is the evidence of maturity. It reveals an understanding that healing is not owed, grace is not earned, and mercy is not deserved. Gratitude turns a blessing into worship.

Psalm 50:23 says, "Whoever offers praise glorifies Me."

What Gratitude Looks Like

Gratitude is not mere politeness. The Samaritan praised with a loud voice, fell on his face, and gave thanks at the feet of Jesus. This was:

- **Public** – He was not ashamed.
- **Physical** – He bowed low.
- **Personal** – He went to Jesus Himself.

Worship is our natural response when we realize what Jesus has done. True gratitude is not silent, passive, or generic. It is loud, humble, and specific.

Lessons at Jesus' Feet

Throughout Luke's Gospel, important moments happen at Jesus' feet:

- Luke 7:47 — A sinful woman weeps and anoints His feet in worship.
- Luke 8:35 — A man once possessed sits clothed and in his right mind.
- Luke 8:41 — Jairus falls at Jesus' feet pleading for his daughter.
- Luke 10:39 — Mary sits at Jesus' feet listening and learning.
- Luke 17:16 — A Samaritan worships in gratitude.

Jesus' feet is the place where humility meets honor, where desperation meets deliverance, where praise meets peace. That is where true disciples want to be.

The Modern Application

Many today are still among the nine. They receive God's provision—health, employment, family—but rarely return in worship.

Faith without gratitude stops short of discipleship. God wants our faith, but He also desires our thanks. Gratitude brings the soul back to its source.

Romans 1:21 indicts the ungodly: "Although they knew God, they did not glorify Him as God, nor were thankful."

True disciples return. They worship. They give thanks.

Faith That Returns

All ten were healed. Only one came back. Jesus' question still rings: *"Where are the nine?"*

Gratitude is more than a feeling—it is a return. It is a choice to glorify God, to bow low, and to say "thank You," not only with words, but with a life devoted to Christ.

May we not be content just to be cleansed. May we, like the Samaritan, return to Jesus and give Him glory.

Let us be the one.

Let us live at His feet.

Discussion Questions

1. Why do you think Jesus asked, "Where are the nine?"
2. What is the difference between being healed and being made whole?
3. Why was it significant that the one who returned was a Samaritan?
4. How does gratitude relate to faith?
5. What prevents people today from returning to give thanks?
6. In what ways does worship demonstrate gratitude?
7. How can we cultivate a grateful heart daily?
8. What blessings have you received without saying, "Thank You, God"?
9. How do you respond when God answers a prayer?
10. Why is it important to spend time at the feet of Jesus?

Additional Verses

1. **Luke 17:17** — "Jesus answered and said, 'Were there not ten cleansed? But where are the nine?'"

2. **Luke 17:13** — "They lifted up their voices and said, 'Jesus, Master, have mercy on us!'"

3. **Leviticus 14** — (The law telling lepers to show themselves to priests.)

4. **Psalm 50:23** — "Whoever offers praise glorifies Me; and to him who orders his conduct aright I will show the salvation of God."

5. **Luke 7:46** — "You did not anoint My head with oil, but this woman has anointed My feet with fragrant oil."

6. **Luke 8:35** — "They went out to see what had happened, and came to Jesus, and found the man from whom the demons had departed, sitting at the feet of Jesus, clothed and in his right mind. And they were afraid."

7. **Luke 10:39** — "She had a sister called Mary, who also sat at Jesus' feet and heard His word."

8. **Romans 1:21** — "Although they knew God, they did not glorify Him as God, nor were thankful, but became futile in their thoughts, and their foolish hearts were darkened."

9. **Luke 13:30** — "Indeed there are last who will be first, and there are first who will be last."

10. **Luke 17:19** — "He said to him, 'Arise, go your way. Your faith has made you well.'"

"Oh, give thanks to the Lord! Call upon His name; Make known His deeds among the peoples! Sing to Him, sing psalms to Him; Talk of all His wondrous works!"

1 CHRONICLES 16:8–9

POLISHING THE PULPIT

09

Why Are You Troubled?

The Risen Lord and the Remedy for Our Fears

Eric Garner

"And He said to them, 'Why are you troubled? And why do doubts arise in your hearts?'"

— **LUKE 24:38**

The Question in the Upper Room

On the evening of Jesus' resurrection, His disciples were gathered in a locked room. They had heard the reports: The women had seen the empty tomb, Peter and John had raced to see it, and some had even spoken with angels. But fear still lingered.

Suddenly, Jesus appeared in their midst and said, "Peace to you" (Luke 24:36). But instead of peace, they were terrified. They thought they were seeing a ghost. So, Jesus asked them, *"Why are you troubled? And why do doubts arise in your hearts?"*

This is more than a rhetorical question. It is a pastoral one—a diagnostis of the heart. Jesus, freshly risen from the grave, addressed the emotional and spiritual condition of His disciples.

This same question echoes into every heart that wrestles with fear, doubt, confusion, or despair. *Why are you troubled?*

Christ Comes to the Troubled

The first thing to notice is that Jesus *comes* to the troubled. He does not avoid the disciples in their fear. He does not wait for them to get it all figured out. He appears to them in the midst of their confusion.

This is consistent with the entire ministry of Jesus. He came to the following:

- A demoniac living in tombs (Mark 5)
- A tax collector hated by his people (Luke 19)
- A woman caught in adultery (John 8)
- A grieving widow in Nain (Luke 7)
- A doubting disciple named Thomas (John 20)

He came to those who were weak, weary, wandering, and wounded. And He comes still.

Jesus said, "Come to Me, all you who labor and are heavy laden, and I will give you rest" (Matthew 11:28). He is drawn to our pain. He meets us in our mess.

What Does It Mean to Be Troubled?

The Greek word translated "troubled" (*tarassō*) means "agitated, stirred, or disturbed." It is the word used when the waters of the pool of Bethesda were stirred (John 5:7), or when Herod was "troubled" by news of a new king (Matthew 2:3).

Jesus uses it to describe the disciples' hearts—unsettled, restless, anxious.

This is not new to the human experience. We are troubled when

- We do not understand what is happening.
- We fear something is out of control.
- We believe that evil is winning.
- We question whether God is truly with us.

Jesus addresses that inner turmoil. He does not merely say, "Do not be troubled." He asks *why*. Because often, our fears rest on lies—and Jesus came to replace lies with truth.

Jesus Answers Our Troubled Hearts

He Offers His Presence

"Behold, My hands and My feet, that it is I Myself" (Luke 24:39). Jesus offered more than a pep talk. He gave Himself. The sight of His scars proved that He had conquered death. The One standing before them was not a ghost—it was their risen Savior.

We too are comforted not by explanations, but by presence. Jesus said, "Lo, I am with you always, even to the end of the age" (Matthew 28:20).

He Offers Peace

Three times in John 20, Jesus says, "Peace to you" (vv. 19, 21, 26). This is more than a greeting—it is a declaration. Peace is now possible because sin has been defeated, death has been conquered, and Jesus is alive.

Romans 5:1 declares, "Having been justified by faith, we have peace with God through our Lord Jesus Christ."

He Offers Purpose

Jesus not only comforted His disciples—He commissioned them. "As the Father has sent Me, I also send you" (John 20:21). He reminded them that their mission was not over. In fact, it had just begun.

Often our troubles intensify when we lose a sense of purpose, but Jesus restores our calling. We are not here to survive. We are here to proclaim.

From Fear to Faith

The disciples' transformation is one of the greatest testimonies to the resurrection. These same men who hid behind locked doors would soon preach openly in the streets. What changed?

- They saw the risen Lord.
- They were filled with the Holy Spirit.
- They understood their mission.

The resurrection did not eliminate all hardship, but it reframed it. They still faced persecution, suffering, and death, but their fear was replaced by boldness. Their sorrow was turned to joy.

Common Causes of Trouble Today

Though we live two thousand years later, our hearts are not so different. Many things still trouble us:

- **Uncertainty about the future** – "What if things do not get better?"
- **Guilt over the past** – "Could God ever forgive me?"
- **Fear of death** – "What happens when I die?"
- **Doubt about God's presence** – "Where is He in this pain?"

Jesus addresses each of these concerns. The empty tomb is His answer. His scars are proof. His words remain: *"Why are you troubled?"*

Replacing Trouble with Trust

Jesus does not just ask *why* we are troubled—He invites us to trust.

Psalm 56:3 says, "Whenever I am afraid, I will trust in You."

Isaiah 26:3 promises, "You will keep him in perfect peace, whose mind is stayed on You, because he trusts in You."

Jesus said, "Let not your heart be troubled; you believe in God, believe also in Me" (John 14:1).

Faith is not the absence of trouble—it is confidence in the presence, power, and promises of Christ.

When Doubts Arise

Jesus not only asked, "Why are you troubled?" but also, "Why do doubts arise in your hearts?" (Luke 24:38).

Doubt is not uncommon, even among the faithful. John the Baptist doubted (Matthew 11:3). Thomas doubted (John 20:25). The disciples doubted.

But Jesus is patient with doubters. He does not scold. He shows. He invites. He proves.

Jude 1:22 says, "Be merciful to those who doubt." Jesus models that mercy. Jude 1:22 reads, "And on some have compassion, making a distinction."

What Does Jesus Want Us to See?

After asking His question, Jesus says, "Behold My hands and My feet" (Luke 24:39). He draws their attention to His scars.

The scars say:

- *"I died for you."*
- *"I conquered sin."*
- *"I am not going anywhere."*

Hebrews 12:2 urges us to fix our eyes on Jesus, "the author and finisher of our faith." Looking to Jesus still calms troubled hearts.

Peace in the Presence of Christ

Jesus' question, "Why are you troubled?" is not a rebuke. It is an invitation to examine what is disturbing us, and then to lay it at His feet.

The risen Christ is not afraid of your doubts. He is not offended by your fears. He welcomes the troubled. He draws near. He shows His hands and His feet.

And He speaks peace.

So next time fear rises, pause and hear His question:

"Why are you troubled?"

Then look to the One who has conquered every fear, and let your heart be still.

Discussion Questions

1. Why do you think Jesus asked, "Why are you troubled?"
2. How does Jesus address fear differently from the world?

"Peace I leave with you, My peace I give to you; not as the world gives do I give to you. Let not your heart be troubled, neither let it be afraid."

JOHN 14:27

3. What can we learn from the way Jesus approached His disciples in Luke 24?

4. What does the word "troubled" reveal about the disciples' emotional state?

5. How does the resurrection change our perspective on suffering?

6. What are some modern "troubles" that affect faith?

7. How can we replace fear with trust?

8. What is the difference between doubt and disbelief?

9. How has Jesus personally comforted you in times of fear?

10. What truths from this story can you apply today?

Additional Verses

1. **Luke 24:38** — "He said to them, 'Why are you troubled? And why do doubts arise in your hearts?'"

2. **John 14:1** — "Let not your heart be troubled; you believe in God, believe also in Me."

3. **Matthew 11:28** — "Come to Me, all you who labor and are heavy laden, and I will give you rest."

4. **Romans 5:1** — "Having been justified by faith, we have peace with God through our Lord Jesus Christ."

5. **Isaiah 26:3** — "You will keep him in perfect peace, whose mind is stayed on You, because he trusts in You."

6. **John 20:21** — "Jesus said to them again, 'Peace to you! As the Father has sent Me, I also send you.'"

7. **Psalm 56:3** — "Whenever I am afraid, I will trust in You."

8. **Hebrews 12:2** — "Looking unto Jesus, the author and finisher of our faith, who for the joy that was set before Him endured the cross, despising the shame, and has sat down at the right hand of the throne of God."

9. **John 20:27** — "He said to Thomas, 'Reach your finger here, and look at My hands; and reach your hand here, and put it into My side. Do not be unbelieving, but believing.'"

10. **Jude 1:22** — "On some have compassion, making a distinction."

How Shall the World Be Salted?

Recovering Our Seasoning Before It Is Too Late

B. J. Clarke

"If the salt loses its flavor, how shall it be seasoned?" —**MATTHEW 5:13**

A Question at the End of a Sermon

Jesus' question in Matthew 5:13 comes on the heels of the greatest sermon ever preached—the Sermon on the Mount. From the opening blessings to the closing warnings, Christ has drawn a portrait of what life in His kingdom looks like. By the time He poses this pointed question, the audience has grown from a few disciples to a multitude. And now He turns their attention to personal responsibility: *How shall the world be salted if we lose our flavor?*

The question is haunting. It is not just poetic; it is practical, personal, and powerful. In our day, with society spiraling into moral and spiritual confusion, it still echoes: If the church loses its influence, who will season the world?

Salt in the Ancient World

To grasp Jesus' question, we need to understand salt's value in His time. The Roman world considered salt so essential that they said, "There are two necessities of life: sun and salt." Roman soldiers were even paid in salt—hence our word "salary," from the Latin *sal*, meaning "salt." The expression "not worth his salt" originated with soldiers who failed to earn their salt pay.

Salt had multiple roles:

- **Flavor enhancing**: It made food taste better, reducing bitterness and boosting sweetness.
- **Preservative**: It drew moisture from meat and inhibited bacterial growth, keeping food from spoiling.
- **Medicinal**: It aided healing, cleansed wounds, and rebalanced electrolytes in the body.
- **Cleansing**: It scrubbed gently but effectively, removing stains and odors.
- **Covenantal**: In Scripture, salt symbolized purity, permanence, and peace (see Numbers 18:19).

Jesus says: "You are the salt of the earth." Not the celebrities. Not the politicians. Not the philosophers. You. Yes, you.

A Warning and a Question

"But if the salt loses its flavor . . . ." In Jesus' time, salt often came from places like the Dead Sea and was mixed with impurities like gypsum or dirt. Through leaching, this salt could lose its potency. It still looked like salt but no longer tasted like it.

So, Jesus asks: "How shall it be seasoned?" How will a bland world recover its flavor if the seasoning itself becomes flavorless? If Christians lose their distinctiveness—if we lose our holiness, our conviction, our joy, our gospel—how will the world be reached?

What It Means to Lose Our Flavor

Losing savor means losing our spiritual distinctiveness. This can happen in a variety of ways:

- **Compromise**: When we blend with the world so completely that no difference can be seen.
- **Apathy**: When we believe but no longer care deeply.
- **Inconsistency**: When our lives contradict our message.
- **Neglect**: When we stop disciplining, evangelizing, and serving.

Jesus is not issuing a chemistry lesson. He is making a kingdom proclamation. We can look like Christians—talk like Christians—even gather like salt in a shaker—but still lack the spiritual force that makes a difference.

The Power of Preserving Influence

Salt restrains decay. So do Christians. We hold back moral rot, not by power or politics, but by presence. Paul told the Philippians they were "in the midst of a crooked and perverse generation, among whom you shine as lights in the world" (Philippians 2:15).

Just one faithful Christian in a workplace, school, or family can serve as a preserving influence. Think of Abraham pleading for Sodom. Just ten righteous men would have saved the city. God's people matter more than we think.

How Christians Are to Be Salt Today

Like salt, we are called to:

- **Enhance the world with grace** (Colossians 4:6)
- **Preserve what is holy** (1 Peter 1:15–16)
- **Heal what is broken** (James 5:14–16)
- **Cleanse with truth and love** (Ephesians 4:15)
- **Create spiritual thirst** (Matthew 5:6)

Jesus' followers are not just seasoning to be admired—they are change agents. We are to transform the environment we are in, not be absorbed by it.

The Church Must Not Go Bland

The church does not need to look more like the world to attract it. It needs to look more like Christ to transform it. When the church becomes entertainment instead of edification, marketing instead of mission, it loses its flavor.

Jesus warns: "It is then good for nothing but to be thrown out and trampled underfoot by men." Salt without savor is useless. Churches without truth are powerless. Disciples without holiness are indistinguishable.

Let us not leave our gatherings, our conferences, or our churches looking like salt but lacking seasoning.

From the Sermon to the Streets

The Sermon on the Mount wasn't meant for notebooks—it was meant for neighborhoods. It is not finished when the preacher says amen. That is when it starts. Jesus gives this salt metaphor right after declaring: "Blessed are you when they revile and persecute you. . . . Rejoice and be exceedingly glad" (Matthew 5:11–12).

Why? Because persecution does not remove our seasoning—it proves it. When we live boldly and faithfully, we preserve and flavor even in adversity.

The Church Is the Only Salt Some Will Ever Taste

We are the only seasoning some people in our families, schools, or communities will ever experience. If we do not bring the gospel, who will? If we do not show Christ's love, who will? We must take our place in the saltshaker of the world.

- **One grain** does little.
- **Many grains together**—a congregation, a family, a movement—can transform communities.

If Nothing Changes, Nothing Changes

If we hear truth but do not live it, nothing changes. If we are moved emotionally but not spiritually, nothing changes. If we are salt that stays in the shaker, nothing changes.

So, we must ask:

- Are we truly flavoring the world?
- Are we seasoning our homes?
- Are we preserving truth where it is being lost?
- Are we creating thirst for righteousness?

The Salt the World Needs

Jesus' question is not rhetorical. It demands an answer—not in words, but in action. The church must be more than a symbol. It must be salt: preserving, purifying, flavoring, healing, and stirring up thirst.

Let us not leave our salt behind at the pew. Let us carry it into the streets, our homes, our workplaces, and the world.

If the salt has lost its savor—*how shall the world be seasoned?*

Let us never find out.

Be the salt.
Be the difference.
Be the seasoning this world desperately needs.

Discussion Questions

1. What specific qualities made salt valuable in Jesus' time?
2. What does Jesus' question, "How shall it be seasoned?" imply about our role?
3. How can Christians lose their "flavor" in today's culture?
4. Why is distinctiveness essential for Christian influence?
5. How does salt both preserve and purify?
6. In what ways can one person be a preserving influence in a community?
7. What are some practical ways we can be "salt" in our workplace or neighborhood?
8. Why is unity among believers important for being salt together?
9. What does "If nothing changes, nothing changes" mean spiritually?
10. What area of your life needs to regain its seasoning power?

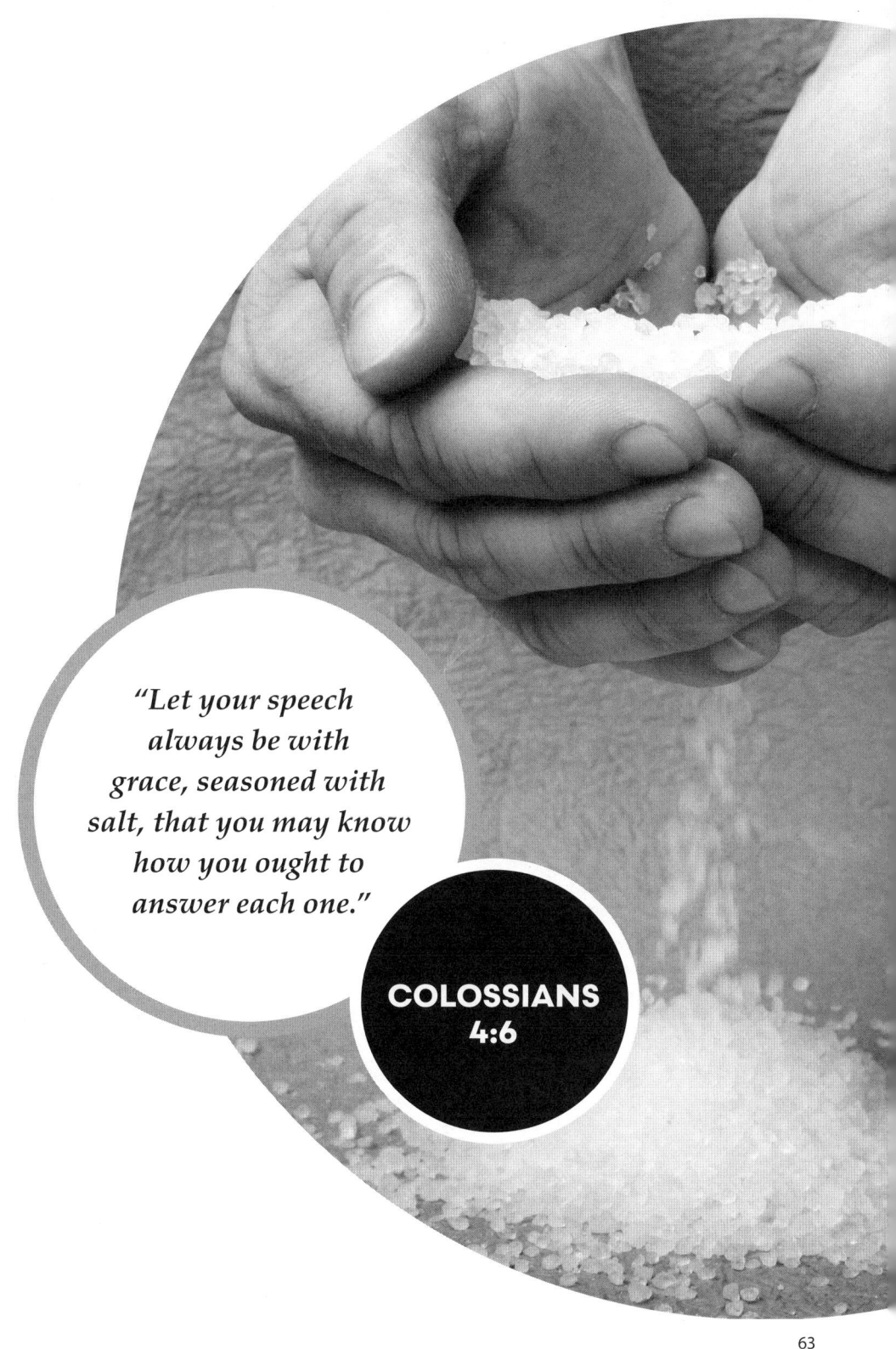

"Let your speech always be with grace, seasoned with salt, that you may know how you ought to answer each one."

COLOSSIANS 4:6

Additional Verses

1. **Matthew 5:13** — "You are the salt of the earth; but if the salt loses its flavor, how shall it be seasoned? It is then good for nothing but to be thrown out and trampled underfoot by men."

2. **Numbers 18:19** — "All the heave offerings of the holy things, which the children of Israel offer to the Lord, I have given to you and your sons and daughters with you as an ordinance forever; it is a covenant of salt forever before the Lord with you and your descendants with you."

3. **Leviticus 2:13** — "Every offering of your grain offering you shall season with salt; you shall not allow the salt of the covenant of your God to be lacking from your grain offering. With all your offerings you shall offer salt."

4. **Colossians 4:6** — "Let your speech always be with grace, seasoned with salt, that you may know how you ought to answer each one."

5. **Philippians 2:15** — "That you may become blameless and harmless, children of God without fault in the midst of a crooked and perverse generation, among whom you shine as lights in the world."

6. **Ephesians 4:15** — "Speaking the truth in love, may grow up in all things into Him who is the head—Christ."

7. **James 5:14–16** — "Is anyone among you sick? Let him call for the elders of the church, and let them pray over him, anointing him with oil in the name of the Lord. And the prayer of faith will save the sick, and the Lord will raise him up. And if he has committed sins, he will be forgiven. Confess your trespasses to one another, and pray for one another, that you may be healed. The effective, fervent prayer of a righteous man avails much."

8. **1 Peter 1:15–16** — "As He who called you is holy, you also be holy in all your conduct, because it is written, 'Be holy, for I am holy.'"

9. **Romans 12:2** — "Do not be conformed to this world, but be transformed by the renewing of your mind, that you may prove what is that good and acceptable and perfect will of God."

10. **Matthew 5:11–12** — "Blessed are you when they revile and persecute you, and say all kinds of evil against you falsely for My sake. Rejoice and be exceedingly glad, for great is your reward in heaven, for so they persecuted the prophets who were before you."

POLISHING THE
PULPIT

My God, My God, Why Have You Forsaken Me?

*Exploring Calvary's Compassion
and Abandonment*

Wendell Winkler

Wendell Winkler was instrumental in the early years of
PTP. He present this lesson at PTP in 2005.

"Woman, behold your son. . . . Behold your mother." —**JOHN 19:26–27**
"My God, My God, why have You forsaken Me?" —**MATTHEW 27:46**

At the Foot of the Cross: Compassion in the Midst of Agony

As the shadow of Calvary lengthened, Jesus, battered and bleeding, lifted His eyes from agony and focused on a small cluster of people. There, near the foot of the cross, stood His mother Mary and the disciple John. In that moment, amidst unspeakable pain, Jesus expressed not anger, not complaint—but compassion.

He spoke seven times from the cross. The first three sayings—spoken while nails pierced His flesh—were for others. He prayed for His executioners. He promised paradise to a dying thief. And now, He tenderly provided for His mother. "Woman, behold your son. Son, behold your mother."

This was not mere sentiment. It was sacrificial love. It reminds us that Jesus did not merely die for the world—He died for people. Individuals. His eyes were

65

never so fixed on heaven that He overlooked the needs at hand. He knew what His mother would need when He was gone.

In the moment when death was inches away, Jesus planned for life to continue—life for Mary, cared for by the faithful John, and a new spiritual relationship forged in the crucible of suffering.

What We Learn from "Behold Your Mother"

Honor for Parents, Even in Pain

Jesus, even in His final breaths, fulfilled the fifth commandment—"Honor your father and your mother" (Exodus 20:12). In a moment when He had every reason to think only of Himself, He entrusted Mary to John's care.

First Timothy 5:4 exhorts believers "to show piety at home and to repay their parents." Christ modeled this perfectly. It was not about convenience; it was about covenant.

Our love for family must be more than sentimental. It must be sacrificial. Our care for those who reared us is not optional—it is spiritual worship.

The Church Needs Standbys, Not Bystanders

Only a few remained at the cross. Most had fled. But John, along with several women, stayed. They were the standbys—those who did not run when things got hard. In every age, the church needs people willing to stand by the Lord when it costs something.

The cross has a separating effect. It reveals who is truly committed. Many profess Christ in comfort, but only a few stay when things get costly.

Love Is Always Personal

Jesus did not instruct a crowd. He did not delegate to an unnamed disciple. He looked directly at Mary. He looked directly at John. "Behold your son . . . your mother." True love is never vague. It is intimate, specific, and sacrificial.

This new relationship, forged in the shadow of the cross, reminds us that God's kingdom family is deeper than biology. John took Mary into his own home "from that hour." The church is a family of faith—and we are called to love one another in practical, ongoing ways.

The Only Question Jesus Asked God

Hours passed. The sun darkened. From the sixth hour to the ninth, darkness fell across the land. And then came the fourth saying—unlike any other statement, before or after: "My God, My God, why have You forsaken Me?"

It is the only recorded time Jesus ever addressed God without calling Him "Father." It is the only question He asked from the cross, and it is the most haunting. This cry, recorded in both Aramaic and translation, is preserved exactly: *"Eli, Eli, lama sabachthani?"* It echoes across centuries from Psalm 22:1.

This was not confusion. Jesus knew the plan. He had prophesied His death. He had set His face like flint to Jerusalem. But in this moment, bearing the sin of the world, He experienced separation from God—a spiritual agony that struck deeper than any nail.

What We Learn from "Why Have You Forsaken Me?"

Life Can Become Bewilderingly Hard

Even for the Son of God, there came a moment of darkness. This validates our own struggles. If Jesus could ask "why," so can we. But note: He did not scream into the void. He addressed *God*. Even in pain, He prayed.

We too must learn to cry *to* God, not just *about* Him. The path of faith sometimes passes through confusion—but faith keeps walking.

The Weight of Sin Is Real

Isaiah 59:2 says, "Your iniquities have separated you from your God." At that moment, Jesus bore our sin (2 Corinthians 5:21), and He experienced that separation—not because of His own wrong, but because He stood in our place.

The just wrath of God was poured out, not on rebels, but on the Redeemer. The holy God cannot overlook sin indefinitely, and at Calvary, Jesus became the sin-bearer. What we deserved, He endured.

Scripture Can Be Our Voice in Suffering

Jesus was quoting Psalm 22:1. In His darkest hour, He reached for Scripture. Let this be our model. When words fail, let the Word speak.

Psalm 22 moves from lament to praise. By quoting its opening line, Jesus invites us to see the whole arc of the psalm—a journey from anguish to victory. Even in despair, hope was on His mind.

God's Silence Does Not Equal His Absence

God did not answer audibly. But the resurrection was coming. The cross is not the end. In our lives, too, God's silence is not always His rejection. His purposes are often beyond our understanding.

Silence does not mean abandonment. Sometimes, in the classroom of suffering, the Teacher is silent while we are being tested. Yet He is present. Always present.

Theological Insights

Christ Was Not a Sinner, But a Sin-Offering

He "bore our sins in His own body on the tree" (1 Peter 2:24). He did not become guilty, but He took our guilt. The abandonment He felt was not deserved—it was substitutionary.

He became the scapegoat, driven outside the camp (Leviticus 16:10), bearing away the iniquity of the people. This was more than physical death—it was spiritual burden.

The Darkness Meant Judgment

From noon to 3:00 p.m., the sun stopped shining. This was no eclipse. It was the judgment of heaven falling upon sin—our sin. Amos 8:9 had predicted a day when the sun would go down at noon. That prophecy came true at Calvary.

Darkness in Scripture often symbolizes judgment (Exodus 10:22; Joel 2:2). The plague of darkness in Egypt preceded deliverance. So too here: This darkness ushered in redemption.

God Turned from Him So He Would Never Turn from Us

Jesus was forsaken so we would never be. Hebrews 13:5 promises, "I will never leave you nor forsake you." He bore our forsakenness to secure our acceptance.

This is the gospel's beauty: The Son cried out so that we might draw near. Because of His abandonment, we have access. Because He was cast out, we are brought in.

Practical Applications

Honor Loved Ones Now

Do not wait to care for family. Jesus used His final moments to provide for His mother. We must be intentional in loving the people God has placed in our lives.

In an age of independence, let us reclaim the beauty of mutual care. Elders are to be honored. Families are to be nurtured. Our love should have hands and feet.

Beware of External Religion

Those who mocked Jesus claimed to be godly. They had religion but no heart. True faith includes compassion.

We must ask: Is our religion a robe or a reality? Are we simply playing the part, or do we truly love Christ and neighbor?

Let Suffering Draw You to Scripture

Jesus quoted a psalm in pain. We can do the same. In distress, turn to the Bible for perspective and hope.

Memorize the Word before you need it, so it will be there when darkness comes. The Word hidden in our hearts becomes a lamp in the valley.

Serve Even in Suffering

Christ served from the cross. We too can serve others even when life hurts. Suffering is not an excuse to stop being Christian—it is an opportunity to show Christ to the world.

Pain can shrink our world—but love expands it. In suffering, look for someone to bless. Like Jesus, see the need in front of you.

From the Cross to Our Hearts

Two sayings. One from love. One from agony. Together, they show us the depth of Christ's care and the weight of His sacrifice. He loved His mother enough to care for her. He loved the world enough to be forsaken for it.

The cross is not just history—it is a mirror. It shows us who we are, what we need, and what God gave. May we never become desensitized to the cost of our salvation.

Let us live in response—not merely with admiration, but with adoration. Let us honor those God has given us, serve through our suffering, and trust in the silence. Because Jesus was forsaken, we are not.

May we never forget the love that stood at Calvary and the silence that shattered heaven—for our sake.

Discussion Questions

1. Why did Jesus entrust Mary to John?
2. What does "Behold your mother" teach us about honoring parents?
3. Why is it important to be a standby instead of a bystander in the faith?
4. Why did Jesus not use the word "Father" in Matthew 27:46?
5. How does Psalm 22 deepen your understanding of the crucifixion?
6. What does it mean that Jesus "became sin" for us?
7. Why do you think the sun darkened during the crucifixion?
8. How should Christians respond when God feels silent?
9. In what ways can we serve others, even during personal suffering?
10. How does Jesus' cry of abandonment strengthen your faith?

Additional Verses

1. **John 19:26–27** — "When Jesus therefore saw His mother, and the disciple whom He loved standing by, He said to His mother, 'Woman, behold your son!' Then He

said to the disciple, 'Behold your mother!' And from that hour that disciple took her to his own home."

2. **Matthew 27:46** — "About the ninth hour Jesus cried out with a loud voice, saying, 'Eli, Eli, lama sabachthani?' that is, 'My God, My God, why have You forsaken Me?'"

3. **Psalm 22:1** — "My God, My God, why have You forsaken Me? Why are You so far from helping Me, and from the words of My groaning?"

4. **Isaiah 59:2** — "Your iniquities have separated you from your God; and your sins have hidden His face from you, so that He will not hear."

5. **2 Corinthians 5:21** — "He made Him who knew no sin to be sin for us, that we might become the righteousness of God in Him."

6. **1 Peter 2:24** — "Who Himself bore our sins in His own body on the tree, that we, having died to sins, might live for righteousness—by whose stripes you were healed."

7. **Amos 8:9** — "'And it shall come to pass in that day,' says the Lord God, 'That I will make the sun go down at noon, and I will darken the earth in broad daylight.'"

8. **Hebrews 13:5** — "Let your conduct be without covetousness; be content with such things as you have. For He Himself has said, 'I will never leave you nor forsake you.'"

9. **1 Timothy 5:4** — "If any widow has children or grandchildren, let them first learn to show piety at home and to repay their parents; for this is good and acceptable before God."

10. **Galatians 2:20** — "I have been crucified with Christ; it is no longer I who live, but Christ lives in me; and the life which I now live in the flesh I live by faith in the Son of God, who loved me and gave Himself for me."

PSALM 23:4

"Though I walk through the valley of the shadow of death, I will fear no evil; for You are with me; Your rod and Your staff, they comfort me."

POLISHING THE
PULPIT

Who Is My Mother and Brethren?

The Priority of the Spiritual Family

B. J. Clarke

"While He was still talking to the multitudes, behold, His mother and brothers stood outside, seeking to speak with Him. Then one said to Him, 'Look, Your mother and Your brothers are standing outside, seeking to speak with You.' But He answered and said to the one who told Him, 'Who is My mother and who are My brothers?' And He stretched out His hand toward His disciples and said, 'Here are My mother and My brothers! For whoever does the will of My Father in heaven is My brother and sister and mother.'"

—MATTHEW 12:46–50

The Family of God: Doing the Will of the Father

If Jesus Christ were to walk into our assembly today and scan the congregation, pointing out those who truly belong to His family, whom would He identify? Would He recognize you? Would He recognize me?

This is no idle question. In a world filled with assumptions about salvation and spiritual identity, the words of Jesus in Matthew 12:50 pierce through the noise with sobering clarity: "Whoever does the will of My Father in heaven is My brother and sister and mother." In that one sentence, He redefined what it means to belong to the family of God—not by blood, culture, or religious heritage, but by obedience.

71

Redefining Family

In Matthew 12:46–50, Jesus was in the middle of teaching when He was interrupted. His biological mother and brothers were standing outside, desiring to speak with Him. The moment might have seemed a minor disruption, but Jesus turned it into a divine teaching opportunity. He asked, "Who is My mother and who are My brothers?" Then He stretched out His hand toward His disciples and declared, "Here are My mother and My brothers! For whoever does the will of My Father in heaven is My brother and sister and mother."

This was not a moment of forgetfulness or emotional detachment. Jesus was not minimizing His earthly relationships—He was magnifying the eternal. The kingdom of God transcends earthly ties. The spiritual family of Christ is comprised of those who obey the will of the Father in heaven.

This declaration echoes Jesus' words in Matthew 7:21: "Not everyone who says to Me, 'Lord, Lord,' shall enter the kingdom of heaven, but he who does the will of My Father in heaven." Not every religious person, not even every person who claims Jesus as Lord, is in the family of God. The key distinction is obedience—doing the Father's will.

The Test of True Kinship

Jesus introduced what we might call a "spiritual DNA test." Just as paternity can be verified through genetic evidence, spiritual sonship is proven by our willingness to do the will of our heavenly Father. A person may believe Jesus is the Christ, may be active in church, and even teach or serve in His name. But unless that person is obedient to all the revealed will of God, he or she does not belong to the family.

In Matthew 7:22–23, Jesus reveals the tragic fate of many religious people on Judgment Day: "Many will say to Me in that day, 'Lord, Lord, have we not prophesied in Your name . . . cast out demons in Your name . . . and done many wonders in Your name?' And then I will declare to them, 'I never knew you; depart from Me, you who practice lawlessness!'" These people had religious credentials but lacked obedient hearts. They called Him "Lord" but did not do what He commanded. Partial obedience, or obedience based on preference, is not submission—it is self-will.

Cafeteria Religion

We live in an age of selective Christianity. Much like a cafeteria line, many approach the Bible and pick and choose what they like, leaving behind the teachings that are uncomfortable, controversial, or personally inconvenient. They say, "I will take a helping of love, a side of grace, and a dessert of heaven. But leave out baptism, church discipline, sacrificial living, and moral purity."

This pick-and-choose theology is not obedience; it is rebellion dressed in religious clothing.

An old story illustrates this well. A father passed away and left instructions for his sons to follow. The will asked them to build a fence in one part of the field, a barn in another, and a well in a specific location. The sons eagerly followed the first two instructions—because they agreed with them. But when it came to digging the well, they disagreed with the father's judgment and dug it elsewhere.

Were they obedient sons? No. True obedience is tested when our will and God's will collide. Obedience that only agrees when convenient is not submission—it is agreement, and it falls short of the surrender Christ demands.

Real-Life Examples of Obedience (or Its Absence)

Let us examine three real-life stories that illustrate how individuals respond when they encounter the will of the Father in Scripture.

Pop Collins – A 92-Year-Old Seeker

In Knoxville, Tennessee, a 92-year-old man named Pop Collins opened his large-print Bible and began reading John 3. When he read Jesus' statement to Nicodemus—"Unless one is born of water and the Spirit, he cannot enter the kingdom of God" (John 3:5)—it stopped him in his tracks. He had been religious for decades, but he had never obeyed this command.

Pop searched the Scriptures and recalled the Ethiopian eunuch in Acts 8. After hearing the gospel preached, the eunuch said, "See, here is water. What hinders me from being baptized?" (Acts 8:36). Pop realized that to be born of water and the Spirit, he too needed to be baptized.

He called his longtime preacher, who tried to explain the verse away, saying the "water" referred to a mother's water breaking during childbirth. But Pop was not buying it. He said, "Then what was the eunuch pointing at when he said, 'Here is water'?" The preacher refused to baptize him.

Undeterred, Pop called multiple churches, asking to be baptized. One by one, they refused, offering him a prayer instead. Finally, through a providential phone call to a hospital, he was connected with a member of the Lord's church. They took him to the building, carried him gently to the baptistry, and immersed him in water for the remission of sins. At 92, Pop became a part of God's family because he did the will of the Father in heaven.

The Porch-Sitter in Etowah

In Etowah, Tennessee, a young preacher handed a gospel meeting flyer to a man sitting on his porch. The man asked, "Aren't you the group that says baptism has something to do with salvation?" The preacher replied carefully, offering biblical explanations. But the man interrupted him: "There ain't no place in the Bible that says baptism saves us!"

The preacher invited him to read 1 Peter 3:21 aloud: "There is also an antitype which now saves us—baptism. . . ." The man read the verse, mouthed the words, paused, and said with trembling hands, "It says it saves us, but I do not believe it. Get off my property."

He saw the will of the Father but rejected it. Why? Perhaps pride. Perhaps tradition. But certainly not submission. He knew what the Bible said and still refused. According to Jesus' test, was he in the family? No—not because someone else judged him unworthy, but because he refused to do the will of the Father.

The Woman at the Kitchen Table

In Noblesville, Indiana, a woman studying the Bible with a gospel preacher slammed her fist on the kitchen table in frustration. She had just read 1 Peter 3:21 and realized she had been misled for years.

"I am mad at myself," she said. "I have owned a Bible for years and never read it all the way through. If I had, I would have seen this verse long ago. And I am mad at every preacher who told me baptism was not necessary. They were wrong!"

That very night, she was baptized for the forgiveness of sins. Her heart was pricked, her will was surrendered, and her soul was added to God's family. That is what it means to be "doers of the word, and not hearers only" (James 1:22).

Can We Understand the Will?

Some object: "But how can we know the will of the Father? I thought it was too mysterious or complex?"

Scripture says otherwise. In Ephesians 5:17, Paul commands us to "understand what the will of the Lord is." In Ephesians 3:4, he says, "When you read, you may understand my knowledge in the mystery of Christ." The Bible was not given to confuse—it was given to reveal.

We can understand it. We must understand it. And once we do, we must obey it. That is what Jesus is teaching in Matthew 12:46–50: The family of God consists of those who hear the word of God and do it (Luke 8:21).

Not Just the Right Name

Claiming the name "Christian" does not make one a child of God. An illustration helps: Imagine a mother loses her child in a crowded mall. She describes her son to the search team: "His name is Joey. He has blond hair, blue eyes, a yellow shirt, brown pants, and a birthmark on his neck."

What if someone brings a child named Joey—but he has red hair, a different outfit, and no birthmark? Would she accept him just because he has the right name? No. She's looking for all the identifying marks.

God is, too.

Someone may have the right name and show some right signs—belief, moral living, religious zeal—but without the new birth (John 3:5), without full obedience to the gospel, they are not yet in the family of God.

Jesus: The Only Way

Jesus said, "I am the way, the truth, and the life. No one comes to the Father except through Me" (John 14:6). And again, "If you do not believe that I am He, you will die in your sins" (John 8:24). Acts 4:12 declares, "Nor is there salvation in any other, for there is no other name under heaven given among men by which we must be saved."

These are not harsh words. They are loving truths spoken by the Savior who died to make salvation possible. If we ignore His clear instructions, we do not just reject doctrine—we reject Him.

Will You Do His Will?

There is still time. The invitation of Christ remains open. If you have heard, believed, repented, confessed, but not yet obeyed the gospel in baptism—then you are standing outside the family. But that can change today.

One young woman, raised in the church building but never obedient, once ran down the aisle when she finally realized her need. She did not wait. She did not deliberate. She obeyed. And heaven rejoiced.

You can do the same. The family of God isn't exclusive, but it is defined. Jesus said, "Whoever does the will of My Father in heaven is My brother and sister and mother." Will you be counted among them?

Discussion Questions

1. How does Jesus' response to His mother and brothers redefine what it means to be part of God's family?

2. Why do you think Jesus emphasizes doing the Father's will, rather than just acknowledging Him as Lord?

3. How can we tell the difference between obeying God and merely agreeing with Him when it is convenient?

4. What can we learn from Pop Collins about persistence in obeying God's word, even late in life?

5. Why is it so difficult for some to accept clear biblical teachings like baptism for salvation?

6. What does it mean to have a "spiritual birthmark" in God's eyes?

7. How should we respond when we discover we have misunderstood or neglected part of God's will?

8. In what ways can selective obedience be more dangerous than outright disbelief?

9. How do Jesus' exclusive claims challenge today's culture of religious pluralism?

10. What attitudes of Cornelius (Acts 10) made him an ideal example of someone who did the will of the Father?

Additional Verses

1. **Matthew 12:50** — "Whoever does the will of My Father in heaven is My brother and sister and mother."

2. **Matthew 7:21** — "Not everyone who says to Me, 'Lord, Lord,' shall enter the kingdom of heaven, but he who does the will of My Father in heaven."

3. **Matthew 7:23** — "I will declare to them, 'I never knew you; depart from Me, you who practice lawlessness!'"

4. **Luke 6:46** — "But why do you call Me 'Lord, Lord,' and not do the things which I say?"

5. **John 3:5** — "Jesus answered, 'Most assuredly, I say to you, unless one is born of water and the Spirit, he cannot enter the kingdom of God.'"

6. **Acts 8:36** — "As they went down the road, they came to some water. And the eunuch said, 'See, here is water. What hinders me from being baptized?'"

7. **1 Peter 3:21** — "There is also an antitype which now saves us—baptism (not the removal of the filth of the flesh, but the answer of a good conscience toward God), through the resurrection of Jesus Christ."

8. **John 14:6** — "Jesus said to him, 'I am the way, the truth, and the life. No one comes to the Father except through Me.'"

9. **John 8:24** — "Therefore I said to you that you will die in your sins; for if you do not believe that I am He, you will die in your sins."

10. **Acts 10:33** — "I sent to you immediately, and you have done well to come. Now therefore, we are all present before God, to hear all the things commanded you by God."

ROMANS 8:16–17

"The Spirit Himself bears witness with our spirit that we are children of God, and if children, then heirs—heirs of God and joint heirs with Christ, if indeed we suffer with Him, that we may also be glorified together."

**PTP books, thumb drives, and
other materials can be purchased
at GladTidingsPublishing.com.**

All proceeds for PTP books go
to help Polishing the Pulpit.

NOTES

NOTES

NOTES

NOTES